ALSO AVAILABLE FROM SHIGERU MIZUKI

Showa: A History of Japan (four-part series)

Kitaro

NonNonBa

Shigeru Mizuki's Hitler

The Birth of Kitaro

Kitaro Meets Nurarihyon

Kitaro and the Great Tanuki War

Kitaro's Strange Adventures

Kitaro the Vampire Slayer

Kitaro's Yokai Battles

The Trial of Kitaro

Tono Monogatari

Story, art, and afterword copyright © 2011, 2022 Shigeru Mizuki/Mizuki Productions. Introduction copyright © 2011, 2022 Frederik L. Schodt. Translation copyright © 2011, 2022 Jocelyne Allen. This edition copyright © 2011, 2022 Drawn & Quarterly. All rights reserved. No part of this book (except small portions for review purposes) may be reproduced in any form without written permission from Shigeru Mizuki/ Mizuki Productions or Drawn & Quarterly. Originally published as *Soin gyokusai seyo!* in 1973. Translation advisor: Brian Allen. Font design: Kevin Huizenga. Drawn & Quarterly also gratefully acknowledges Presspop Inc. and Maki Hakui for their invaluable assistance with the publication of this book.

drawnandquarterly.com

ISBN 978-1-77046-630-2 | First paperback edition: April 2011 | Second paperback edition: August 2022. Printed in Malaysia | 10 9 8 7 6 5 4 3 2 1

Cataloguing data available from Library and Archives Canada.

Published in the USA by Drawn & Quarterly, a client publisher of Farrar, Straus and Giroux. Published in Canada by Drawn & Quarterly, a client publisher of Raincoast Books. Published in the United Kingdom by Drawn & Quarterly, a client publisher of Publishers Group UK.

Onward Towards Our Noble Deaths

Shigeru Mizuki

Translation by
Jocelyne Allen

DRAWN &
QUARTERLY

INTRODUCTION

Frederik L. Schodt

When I heard that one of Shigeru Mizuki's stories was about to be published in English, my first thought was: Finally! There has been an explosion in the number of translated manga titles in the last twenty years—so much so that some fans can be forgiven for thinking they now have access to most everything ever published in Japan. But there are still many famous works with a universal quality, done by extraordinarily talented artists which, for various and mysterious reasons, remain unknown in North America. Foremost among them until recently, to my way of thinking, has been the work of Shigeru Mizuki.

As I write this, Shigeru Mizuki is nearly ninety years old, living on the outskirts of Tokyo. Unlike most artists, whose auras start to fade with the passing years, he has only grown brighter, as new generations discover his work, and older generations discover new aspects of the man they thought they knew so well. Among the pantheon of legendary manga artists in Japan, Mizuki stands out not only for his longevity, but also for his originality. When discussing him, critics rarely talk about how he resembles other artists because it is difficult to compare him to anyone else. He started drawing manga before most artists alive today were born, and he has already outlived many pioneering (and younger) luminaries of manga's golden age, such as Osamu Tezuka, Fujiko F. Fujio, and Shôtarô Ishinomori.

Mizuki was born Shigeru Mura in 1922, and raised on the isolated western seaboard of Japan. He exhibited a precocious drawing ability as a child. Much later, after the war, he briefly attended the prestigious Musashino Art University in Tokyo, but he fortunately did not become mired in artistic orthodoxy. Today one of the hallmarks of many of his manga stories is his use of highly realistic, detailed backgrounds, while rendering human characters in quirky, "cartoony" shapes.

From an early age, Mizuki had a voracious curiosity about the world and about life, and an independent streak. As a child, a local woman he called *non-non bâ*, or "Auntie Non-non," often took care of him, and helped him develop a passionate interest in the spirit world, especially in local tales of *yôkai*. Sometimes translated as goblins and ghosts in the animistic world view of Japanese people, yôkai often resemble the trolls of northern Europe, for they are closely linked with local natural phenomena and objects. Mizuki would eventually make yôkai his trademark manga subjects, and become Japan's foremost yôkai popularizer. As a self-declared yôkai researcher, he would also look beyond Japan, and travel to exotic locales around the world to learn about the supernatural beliefs of other cultures.

In the early postwar period, before entering the manga mainstream, Mizuki worked for a time drawing for the *kamishibai* or "paper-play" market—an inexpensive form of street entertainment in the days before television wherein raconteurs embroidered tales with a sequence of illustrated panels. Kamishibai have largely vanished from modern Japan, but there is currently a renewed interest in their connection to modern manga. Not coincidentally,

Mizuki and some of his kamishibai work was recently introduced in the United States in 2010, in Eric P. Nash's lavishly illustrated book, *Manga Kamishibai*. But Mizuki also drew stories for the manga pay-library market—a series of for-profit libraries that lent manga (and books) for a small fee to entertainment-starved readers. His debut work, published in paperback form in 1957 when he was already thirty-three years old, was titled *Rocketman*.

Mizuki's first real commercial success came around 1965, when he drew a story for boys called *Terebi-kun* [TV kid], about a young boy who discovers how to enter his TV set, steal the products displayed on commercials and give them to his poorer, real-world friends. And thereafter, Mizuki began to win the hearts of Japan, especially with his yôkai stories. He drew heavily on Japanese spirit traditions, but the paranormal world he depicted was completely his own, and the yôkai that populated it were, rather than scary, remarkably bizarre and endearing. Kitarô, his most famous creation, in the series *Ge ge ge no Kitarô* [Kitarô the Spooky], was born of a family of ghost-goblins, the last of their kind on earth, who live among ordinary humans. His parents "die," but the father's eyeball survives (with little arms and legs) and becomes Kitarô's guardian. Kitarô has only one eye, so the father's eye sometimes hides in Kitarô's eye socket. Children absolutely loved this weirdness, and as a result *Ge ge ge no Kitarô* was animated for television in 1968. Today, it is probably safe to say, that in the minds of most young Japanese, Mizuki's yôkai characters and stories have supplanted the original folk-tales and legends that inspired them. It would be hard to exaggerate their popularity.

In 2009, I finally visited Sakaiminato, the little town on the Japan Sea coast where Mizuki grew up. Here, he has been nearly deified, for the train line that runs between the Yonago city and Sakaiminato is now named after his yôkai characters and decorated with their images. And in the town of Sakaiminato there is a section called "Mizuki Road," where the street is lined with over a hundred bronze statues of his yôkai characters, a museum dedicated to him, and stores selling Mizuki and yôkai-themed trinkets. There is even a bronze statue of Mizuki himself, with one of his more famous and typically idiosyncratic recommendations to the world: "Be lazy."

Fascination with Mizuki and his characters has been propelled in recent years by two television series broadcast on the public channel, NHK. The first was an award-winning series in 1991 and 1992, based on one of his stories about "Auntie Non-non," who taught him about the spirit world. The second aired in 2010 and was also hugely popular. Titled *Ge ge ge no nyôbô* [Ge ge ge's wife], it was based on a book by his wife, about her life with her unusual husband.

Yet no matter how popular and commercialized Mizuki and his yôkai world becomes, he always stands apart from other successful manga artists. In large part, this is because of his life experience. Mizuki was an active combatant in World War II, and this fact is always driven home upon meeting him because his left arm is missing.

Mizuki was drafted into the Imperial Army in 1943 and sent to Rabaul, on the island of New Britain, in what is now part of Papua New Guinea. It was one of the worst places to be sent in the war, and quickly became a showcase for some of the worst aspects of the Imperial Army. As one of the lower-ranking, late arrivals in a hierarchical and feudalistic command structure, Mizuki was constantly beaten by his superiors. While on sentry duty in the field one day, his detachment was completely wiped out in an attack by Australians and native forces. Mizuki made a harrowing escape alone back to Japanese lines, only to be reprimanded by his superiors

for losing his rifle, and (in Imperial Army style) for surviving. He later lost his arm during a raid by Allied airplanes, when he was badly wounded. After lingering on the verge of death, and battling malaria, he was eventually nursed back to health.

During this time Mizuki developed a deep affection for the natives of New Guinea, and he claims to have realized that a spirit force was guiding his life. Had he not been out of commission, he probably would not have survived the war. In a fairly famous incident, a unit to which he would have been attached was sent out on a *banzai* [suicide] charge, but miraculously survived. Since the men's "glorious death" had already been reported to headquarters, it was sent back to the front with orders not to return alive.

These personal experiences provide the real punch for Mizuki's war stories, which are far less well known in Japan than his yôkai work. Many have an anti-war theme, commiserate with the plight of the average soldier, and may be a way for him to exorcize his own personal demons. The same burning spirit also pervades a remarkable 2000-page manga documentary work that he created in 1994 about Japan's turbulent and controversial history during the reign of Emperor Hirohito from 1925–1989.

Of Mizuki's war stories, I have always believed that this 1973 *gekiga, Sôin Gyokusai Seyo!* [Onward Towards Our Noble Deaths] is one of his best. It is Mizuki's own telling, in dramatic manga style, of the fate of the aforementioned doomed unit in New Guinea. In the story's gruesome detail, in the contrast between realistic and "cartoony" art, and in Mizuki's obvious anger over the way arrogant officers squandered the lives of their men, I think it is one of the most powerful anti-war comics ever created.

And I am overjoyed that Drawn & Quarterly has decided to publish it.

Frederik L. Schodt
February 2011
San Francisco, California

Frederik L. Schodt is an award-winning author of numerous non-fiction books on Japan, and a well-known translator. In 2009, the emperor of Japan awarded him the Order of the Rising Sun, Gold Rays with Rosette, for his work introducing Japanese modern popular culture to the United States. In 2017 he was also given the prestigious Japan Foundation Award. His latest book is My Heart Sutra: A world in 260 characters, *published by Stone Bridge Press. His website is www.jai2.com.*

CHARACTERS

PLATOON LEADER MIZUMOTO
SECOND LIEUTENANT

COMPANY COMMANDER
CAPTAIN

BATTALION COMMANDER TADOKORO
MAJOR

HONDA, LEADER OF SQUAD NO. 3
SERGEANT

KAWAKITA, LEADER OF SQUAD NO. 2
CORPORAL

YOSHIDA, LEADER OF SQUAD NO. 1
CORPORAL

MARUYAMA
PRIVATE SECOND CLASS

NOGAMI
ACTING CORPORAL

OKUYAMA, LEADER OF SQUAD NO. 4
LANCE-CORPORAL

MIURA
PRIVATE SECOND CLASS

KAGEYAMA
PRIVATE SECOND CLASS

YOKOI
CORPORAL

OGAWA
PRIVATE FIRST CLASS

CORPSMAN KAMIYA
ACTING CORPORAL

KAYAMA
PRIVATE SECOND CLASS

KOBAYASHI
PRIVATE SECOND CLASS

NAKAMOTO
PRIVATE SECOND CLASS

SAKAIDA
PRIVATE SECOND CLASS

AKASAKI
PRIVATE SECOND CLASS

KOJIMA
PRIVATE FIRST CLASS

KANEDA
PRIVATE FIRST CLASS

HOMU
MILITARY POLICE LIEUTENANT

KITAZAKI, LEADER OF PLATOON NO. 3 SECOND LIEUTENANT

YAMAGISHI, LEADER OF PLATOON NO. 1 SECOND LIEUTENANT

DIVISION COMMANDER
LIEUTENANT-GENERAL

CHIEF OF STAFF
COLONEL

KIDO, STAFF
LIEUTENANT-COLONEL

DR. ISHIYAMA
MEDICAL LIEUTENANT

KIRIMOTO
PRIVATE FIRST CLASS

MORITA
PRIVATE FIRST CLASS

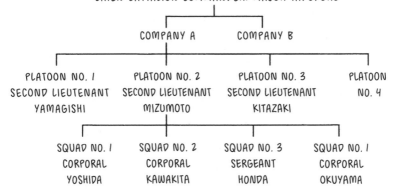

BAIEN BATTALION COMMANDER: MAJOR TADOKORO

COMPANY A — COMPANY B

PLATOON NO. 1
SECOND LIEUTENANT
YAMAGISHI

PLATOON NO. 2
SECOND LIEUTENANT
MIZUMOTO

PLATOON NO. 3
SECOND LIEUTENANT
KITAZAKI

PLATOON
NO. 4

SQUAD NO. 1
CORPORAL
YOSHIDA

SQUAD NO. 2
CORPORAL
KAWAKITA

SQUAD NO. 3
SERGEANT
HONDA

SQUAD NO. 1
CORPORAL
OKUYAMA

TAK

TAK

TAK

TAK

TAK

SAYING IT'S FOR THE GOOD OF OUR COUNTRY
FOOL VOLUNTEERING
FOR THAT ROTTEN ARMY
LEAVING SWEET SUE BEHIND IN TEARS

FORCED AWAKE AT THE CRACK OF DAWN
SWABBING AND SWEEPING
PUSHED AROUND BY FOOLS ABOVE HIM
LONG DAYS SPENT IN TEARS*

*LYRICS FROM A JAPANESE WAR SONG, "KAWAII SU-CHAN."

NOT EVEN TIME TO SCARF DOWN SOME BREAD
AND THE HORN FOR LIGHTS OUT IS SOUNDING
A STRAW MATTRESS BARELY LONG ENOUGH
HERE IS THE LAND OF OUR DREAMS

FAR FROM THE SEA AND MOUNTAINS
AND NOT EVEN A SINGLE VISITOR
THE SWEET DELIGHT OF
SWEET SUE'S SWEET LETTERS

KOKOPO, NEW BRITAIN

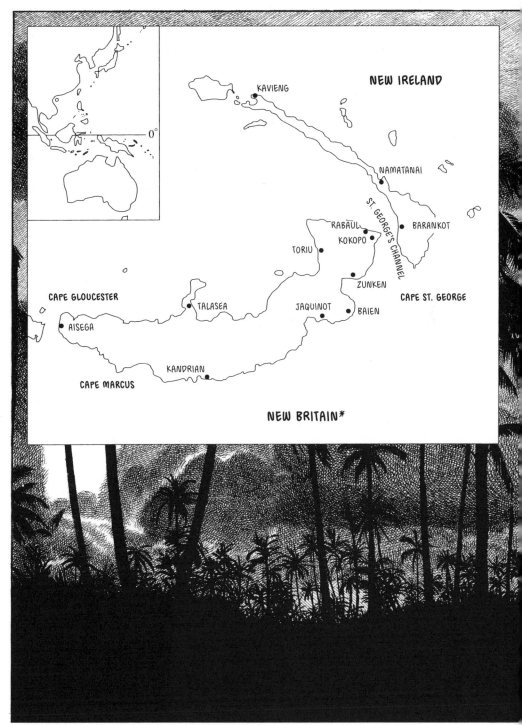

NEW IRELAND

KAVIENG

NAMATANAI

BARANKOT

ST. GEORGE'S CHANNEL

RABAUL
KOKOPO

TORIU

ZUNKEN

CAPE ST. GEORGE

CAPE GLOUCESTER

TALASEA

JAQUINOT

BAIEN

AISEGA

KANDRIAN

CAPE MARCUS

NEW BRITAIN*

*NEW BRITAIN IS AN ISLAND IN THE PAPUA NEW GUINEAN ARCHIPELAGO.

19

I HEARD THEY HAVE PAPAYA TREES WHERE WE'RE HEADED.

OH, CORPORAL NOGAMI!

HEY! WHAT ARE YOU GUYS DOING?

I ALWAYS WANTED TO GO SOME-WHERE LIKE THAT.

I GUESS IT'S LIKE HEAVEN THERE.

BUT MIURA'S STILL HERE.

EVERYONE?

GO ON, GET OVER THERE.

EVERYONE ELSE'S GONE TO THE BROTHEL.

SON OF A BITCH!

WHAT D'YA MEAN, MIURA'S STILL HERE?

...OH.

MIURA'S ALREADY BEEN TO THE BROTHEL THREE TIMES. HE HAS A RIGHT TO BE WORN OUT.

WHHHAAP

THEN, SIR, MARUYAMA AND AKASAKI ARE OFF TO THE BROTHEL.

YES, SIR.

WHEN I TELL YOU TO GO, YOU GO. THE PLACE'S OPEN 'TIL FIVE.

SHIT, JUST FIVE MINUTES 'TIL THEY CLOSE.

THE ONLY DAY WE GET OFF AND WE'RE RUNNING AROUND.

GOOD.

LOOK AT THIS LINE!

HEY! HURRY UP IN THERE!

WE'LL BE HERE ALL NIGHT.

GUYS, IT'S FIVE NOW, SO WE'RE CLOSED FOR THE DAY.

THIRTY SECONDS PER PERSON, YOU KNOW!

MY BODY CAN'T TAKE ANY MORE, HON.

NO, C'MON! IT'S FOR YOUR COUNTRY!

STAY OPEN A LITTLE LONGER!

WE HAVE TO STAY ON THIS ISLAND AND DIE, YOU KNOW!

BUT YOU'RE HEADED HOME IN A COUPLE DAYS ON THE HOSPITAL SHIP.

HEH HEH HEH HEH

I'LL JUST TOUCH, OKAY?

C'MON, GIRLS, THERE'S JUST SEVENTY OF US LEFT. HOLD ON A LITTLE LONGER!

HEH
HEH
HEH
HEH

I'LL JUST LICK.

I AM*

*"PROSTITUTE'S LAMENT" WAS SUNG BY SOLDIERS DURING THE WAR; NO RECORDINGS OF IT REMAIN.

ALL TOGETHER!

A BLOSSOM THAT FALLS IN THE RED LIGHT DISTRICT

WILTING IN THE DAY BLOOMING AT NIGHT

24

MOST OF US GOT NOTHING BUT THE "PROSTITUTE'S LAMENT."

FIVE MINUTES LEFT— MAYBE TWO OR THREE GUYS COULD'VE GOTTEN SOME, BUT SEVENTY OR SO WERE WAITING THERE.

...SAY, HOW WAS IT YESTERDAY?

HUH, TOO BAD.

BUT MIURA, YOU DID IT THREE TIMES!

ME, TOO.

NOW YOU'LL DIE A VIRGIN.

YOU HAD YOUR HEAD STUCK UP YOUR ASS.

FALL IN!

I DIDN'T GO THREE TIMES.

WHAT THE HELL ARE YOU TALKING ABOUT?

I THOUGHT WE WERE SHIPPING OUT.

NUMBERS!

TWO!

ONE!

THE COLONEL'S CALLED EVERYONE IN. MOVE OUT!

SALUTE TO THE FRONT!

SALUTE!

ATTEN-TION!

I AM LIEUTENANT-COLONEL TADOKORO. I WILL COMMAND THIS BATTALION IN BAIEN.

WHEN THE GREAT DAI-NANKO* FOUGHT THE REBELS AT MINATO RIVER, FIVE HUNDRED BRAVE MEN DIED IN BATTLE ALONGSIDE HIM.

*SEE NOTES PAGE 366.

WE WILL BE MOVING OUT FOR BAIEN THIS EVENING.

GENTLEMEN, FIGHT COURA-GEOUSLY AND WITH HONOR!

ASSEMBLED HERE TODAY, WE ARE JUST LIKE THOSE FIVE HUNDRED.

SALUTE TO THE FRONT!

KLAK
KLAK

PRESENT ARMS!

OUR PLATOON WILL OCCUPY BAIEN AS THE ADVANCE PARTY.

CHAK
CHAK

FIX BAYONETS!

CHARGE!

PREPARE TO LAND AND FACE THE ENEMY!

WE HAVE TAKEN THIS PLACE WITHOUT BLOODSHED!

IS THERE EVEN ANY-ONE HERE?

JESUS, IT'S QUIET.

34

ACTUALLY, WE
WERE NOT THAT
FAR FROM
PARADISE...

RAIN IN BAIEN

THIS RAIN'S NEVER GONNA STOP.

ME?

HE SAID 'MESS DUTY,' MARUYAMA.

MESS DUTY!

36

PSSSHH

WHHAAAP

QUIT LOAFING! GET YOUR ASS OUT THERE!

NOT 'OKAY'!

OKAY.

THERE'S RICE STUCK IN HERE. YOU GOTTA WASH IT BETTER THAN THIS.

THUNK

THEY SURE DO.

THEY REALLY STICK IT TO US ROOKIES.

THUMP

GO DO IT AGAIN!

MAYBE YOU SHOULD SEE THE DOC.

I FEEL REALLY FEVERISH.

PSSSHH

GREAT.

ALL RIGHT, THE RICE IS DONE.

"WE CANNOT LET THE WEATHER STOP OUR CAMP CONSTRUCTION."

"ALTHOUGH THE RAINY SEASON IS WELL UNDERWAY..."

I'VE GOT OUR ORDERS FROM THE CAPTAIN.

EVERYBODY, LISTEN UP!

YES, SIR!

FIRST SECTION!

AND THE ENEMY COULD SHOW UP ANYTIME NOW.

WE'RE DIGGING HOLES.

THIRD SECTION— OH, YOU'RE WITH ME.

SECOND SECTION! PUT 'EM IN PLACE!

GO GET SOME PALM TREES.

ANY QUESTIONS?

FOURTH SECTION, GO GET SOME RATIONS.

NO, SIR!

39

OOPH, THIS THING'S HEAVY

SQUICK

THUD
CRACK

YOU OKAY?

WHAT HAPPENED?

CRAP! OGAWA!

SERGEANT HONDA!

NGGH

NGGH

HIS ARM'S BROKEN.

40

HMM.

WONDER IF WE CAN EAT THAT FRUIT OVER THERE.

CHOMP

IF WE DIE HERE...

NOPE! TOO BITTER.

PLEH

I'D PROB'LY TAKE THE FOOD.

I'D GO FOR THE PUSSY.

WOULD YOU RATHER EAT OR FUCK?

GIVE US A HAND.

WE'VE ONLY BROUGHT IN FIVE TREES SINCE THIS MORNING.

YOU GUYS ARE REALLY SOMETHING.

WE'RE JUST BARELY HANGING ON IN THE FACE OF DEATH.

NO CAN DO.

SHUT UP—YOU GUYS ARE TOUGHER THAN ME.

IT'S ALL I CAN DO TO STAY ON MY FEET.

FWOOP

WHADDAYA MEAN 'JINX'?

OWOWOW! DON'T JINX ME LIKE THAT!

HEY, KOBAYASHI! YOU TRYING TO PULL AN OGAWA?

OGAWA DIED THIS MORNING.

WELL, YOU WON'T DIE OF RING-WORM.

NO, I'VE GOT RINGWORM EVERYWHERE.

THAT WAS FAST. YOU'RE PROB'LY NEXT.

THE DENGUE FEVER?

45

THAT BALD BASTARD!

IT'S PRACTICALLY A VACATION.

HE'S WATCHING THE BOATS AT THE WAR-ANGOE RIVER.

IT'S TOO BAD ABOUT OGAWA, BUT KAGEYAMA'S GOT IT PRETTY SWEET.

WELL, THEY HAVE TO FEED US PORK OR SOMETHING GOOD SOME-TIMES.

PORK!!

THERE'S TALK THAT WE'LL GET PORK FOR NEW YEAR'S*.

AND HERE I AM, TOO HUNGRY TO DO ANYTHING.

*SEE NOTES PAGE 366.

ORDERS FOR TOMORROW.

NO, SIR!

ANY QUES-TIONS?

MARUYAMA, SAKAIDA, CATCH A PIG FOR NEW YEAR'S AND BRING IT OVER TO THE COOKS AT HQ.

HEY, YOU'RE FROM MY TOWN, RIGHT?

YEAH.

WE FINALLY ESCAPED FROM BASE BUILDING, HUH?

NOW THAT YOU MENTION IT, WE SHIPPED OUT TOGETHER.

THEY'RE PRETTY GOOD RAW, YOU KNOW.

JUST ONCE, I'D LIKE TO EAT UNTIL I'M FULL.

POTATOES?

I HEARD THERE'S POTATOES ON THE OTHER SIDE OF THE WARANGOE.

LET'S GET GOING AND GET THAT PIG!

YES, SIR!

EVERYONE HERE?

CAN'T WAIT FOR THAT FEAST.

47

YOU MEAN A PIG?

WE'LL DEFINITELY GET ONE.

EITHER WAY, THE COLONEL SAID CATCH ONE.

ARE THERE REALLY PIGS HERE?

HEY, KAGEYAMA, WE'RE COMING!

I HEARD SOME- THING ABOUT ALLIGATORS IN THE RIVER.

ARE WE CROSSING THE WARANGOE RIVER?

HOW MANY ARE YOU?

THE BOAT IS STARTING TO FALL APART, SO ONLY TWO OF YOU CAN GO AT ONCE.

THEN I GUESS IT'S TWO AT A TIME.

LET'S GET OVER THERE AND EAT SOME OF THOSE POTATOES!

OKAY.

YOU WANNA GO NEXT?

I'VE ALWAYS LOVED POT-ATOES, EVER SINCE I WAS A KID.

ME...

HAH HAH HAH

THEY'RE PRETTY GOOD RAW, RIGHT?

WHAT HAPPENED TO SAKAIDA?

WAS HE EATEN BY AN ALLIGATOR?

I THINK HIS HAT FELL OFF. HE WAS REACHING OUT TO GRAB IT AND THEN...

HMM, I WONDER WHAT HAPPENED... I WAS FOCUSED ON DIGGING FOR GOLD.

WHICH MEANS NO TIME FOR PIG HUNTING.

WE NEED EVERYONE HERE. WE'LL HAVE TO LOOK FOR HIM.

YOU'RE RIGHT.

AN ALLIGATOR WOULD'VE MADE MORE NOISE.

THEY SEARCHED TO THE UPPER REACHES OF THE RIVER, BUT FOUND NO TRACE OF SAKAIDA. NIGHT FELL AND THE SEARCH WAS CALLED OFF.

IT'S TRUE.

SOMEONE SAID YOU SHOT AT THE GATOR, BUT YOU MISSED.

THAT'S REALLY SCARY, HUH?

I HEARD IT DIDN'T EVEN MAKE ANY NOISE.

ALL RIGHT, GUYS, TOMORROW... MARUYAMA, YOU'RE DRAWING PLAYING CARDS* FOR THE CAPTAIN.

LISTEN UP!

*SEE NOTES PAGE 366.

YES, SIR!

FIRST SECTION, YOU'RE ON BARRACKS BUILDING.

YES, SIR.

IT'S BEEN A WHILE SINCE IT'S BEEN THIS NICE OUT.

OKAY, SIR.

SAY, WILL YOU DO MY PORTRAIT?

GOOD.

MARUYAMA REPORTING, SIR. HERE TO DRAW SOME CARDS.

WHAT ARE YOU TALKING ABOUT?

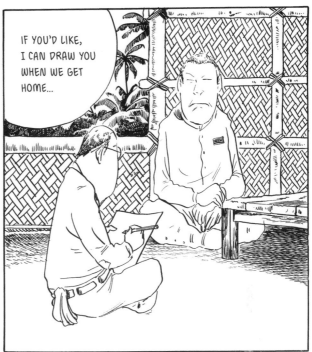

IF YOU'D LIKE, I CAN DRAW YOU WHEN WE GET HOME...

WHEN WE GET BACK TO JAPAN...

THIS IS A PICTURE OF MY FAMILY.

?

TALK SENSE, BOY. NONE OF US ARE LEAVING HERE ALIVE.

THAT'S RIGHT.

YOUR FAMILY RUNS A LUMBER SHOP, SIR?

YES. THERE'LL BE SOME KIND OF MARK IF YOU JUST REPAIR THEM, MAKING IT OBVIOUS WHICH CARD IS WHICH.

YOU WANT ME TO REDRAW ALL OF THEM, SIR?

HERE, THESE CARDS ARE SO WORN OUT I CAN'T USE THEM ANY- MORE.

IT'S LUNCH.

WHAT'RE YOU DOIN' HERE?

UNDERSTOOD, SIR. I'LL GET TO WORK.

YES, SIR.

YOU HAVE TO SAY SOMETHING THE DAY BEFORE IF YOU ARE GOING TO EAT AT HQ.

OOPH

WHHHAAP

BIT LATE FOR THAT!

SO MY LUNCH IS JUST A SLAP...

HEY! KAGEYAMA!

POTATOES!!

KEEP THIS TO YOURSELF, BUT WE GOT SOME POTATOES OVER HERE.

COMING!

WELL, GET IN.

I'M SO HUNGRY, I CAN'T THINK.

HELP
YOURSELF.

MNCH
MNCH

WOW! WITH THIS
MANY POTATOES,
I CAN NOW DIE A
HAPPY MAN!

SOMETHING
COMES
FLOATING
ALONG.

JUST WHEN I
WAS THINKING
IT STANK LIKE
THE DEAD...

AH!

ALLIGATORS DO BURY THEIR FOOD IN THE MUD AND EAT IT ONCE IT ROTS A BIT, SO...

IT HAS TO BE SAKAIDA. SO HE WAS EATEN BY A GATOR.

IT'S THE LOWER HALF OF A SOLDIER!

AND HE REALLY STINKS, HUH?

AND NOW HE'S IN THIS SAD STATE.

WE JOINED UP AT THE SAME TIME, YOU KNOW.

LET'S WASH HIM BEFORE WE BRING HIM BACK.

PSSSSSH

PSSH

PSSH

HARD LABOUR AND A FEW SLAPS

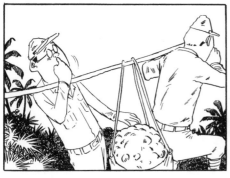

QUIT
SLACKING
OFF!

WHAT
ARE YOU
DOIN'?

HE'S WAY TOO WOUND UP.

WHAT'S SERGEANT HONDA'S PROBLEM?

USELESS PIECE OF CRAP.

YESSIR!

THE ANGLE HERE'S ALL WRONG!

WE'LL BE SHOOTING AT THE ENEMY FROM THESE TRENCHES.

AND WHAT ARE YOU MEN DOING?

WHHHAAP

THE ENEMY'S GONNA BE HERE SOON. WHAT THE HELL ARE YOU THINKING?

'YES, SIR' DOESN'T CUT IT!

YES, SIR!

YOU SAID IT!

HE'S PROB'LY AN ORPHAN FROM HOKKAIDO*.

A REAL BEAR.

WHAT AN ASS.

*SEE NOTES PAGE 366.

WHAT THE HELL ARE YOU YAKKING ABOUT OVER THERE?

AND HE PRACTICALLY KILLED OGAWA.

HE'S DONE NOTHING BUT SLAP US SINCE WE GOT HERE.

WHEW. TIME TO SLEEP— FINALLY.

KREE KREE

YOU MAGGOTS AREN'T PULLING YOUR WEIGHT.

AGGH

ROOKIES TO THE FRONT!

ANY QUES- TIONS?

WHHAAAP

WHHAAAAP

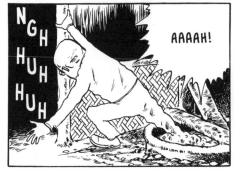

NGH HUH HUH

AAAAH!

SCHLUP

CHRIST, IT'S STICKY!

GAH! MY SHOE!

POP

SEE ME LIKE THIS...

IF THE SERGEANT OR ANY OF THE VETS...

SLIMY

PLOSH

I'LL JUST USE THIS RICE BUCKET.

HAH HAH HAH

OKAY! WATER! HERE'S SOME WATER!

62

THAT WAS NO FUN.

WHEW.

SPLISH SPLISH SPLISH

NUMBERS!

ROLL CALL!

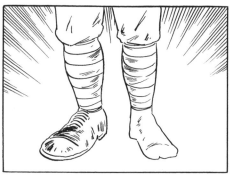

ONE TWO THREE

I SLIPPED AND FELL INTO THE RIVER... AND...

UH, YES, UM, IT—

YOUR SHOE...

DAMMIT. SLAPPED FIRST THING IN THE MORNING.

DAMMIT.

'CAUSE YOU'RE SO DAMNED CARELESS!

WHHHAAP

EVEN IF THEY WASHED IT, THE SHIT FROM LAST NIGHT SHOULD STILL BE IN THERE.

2.

HEY! HAND OVER THE RICE—I'M SERVING.

SHIT FOR THE SERGEANT...

THIS'LL BE GOOD.

GRUB'S ON!

IT DEFINITELY LOOKS BROWNISH.

64

HEY, MARUYAMA.

I TOLD YOU TO EAT MY RICE. YOU NOT GONNA EAT IT?

SORRY, SIR?

I ALREADY ATE AT HQ, SO YOU GO AHEAD AND EAT MY RICE.

MNCH MNCH MNCH

CHOMP

YES, SIR! THANK YOU VERY MUCH, SIR.

STILL HAVEN'T FOUND YOUR SHOE?

THOK

HUH?

CAN'T BE HELPED.

UH, NO SIR.

YEAH.

SERGEANT HONDA'S ALL RIGHT SOMETIMES, HUH?

SIR, THIS IS TOO MUCH.

SHUT UP AND PUT IT ON!

AAAWK AWK

HE HAS A BOY IN GRADE FIVE AND A GIRL WHO'S ALMOST THREE.

I HEARD...

YES, SIR.

SERGEANT HONDA, YOUR SHOES...

THE ORDER'S COME DOWN FROM DIVISION HQ FOR THE MATSUYAMA CAMP MEN TO HEAD OUT THIS MONTH.

HA HA HA HA!

I DECIDED TO GO BAREFOOT FROM NOW ON.

UNDERSTOOD, SIR. MY MEN AND I WON'T LET YOU DOWN.

SINCE THE PIG HUNT FOR NEW YEAR'S FAILED, WE ARE TO GO FISHING WITH OUR GRENADES.

LISTEN UP!

NO SIR

THE REST OF YOU ARE BASE BUILDING. ANY QUESTIONS?

NAKAMOTO, KAYAMA. YOU ARE FISHING.

WHHHHAAAAP

GULP

ROOKIES, FALL IN!

THANK YOU, SIR!

NEW RECRUITS ARE LIKE TATAMI MATS: THE MORE YOU BEAT THEM, THE BETTER THEY ARE.

YOU GET THE MESSAGE?

OF COURSE.

IF WE CATCH SOMETHING, LET'S JUST SLICE IT UP INTO SASHIMI AND CHOW DOWN.

HOOEEE! HA HA!

YOU WANT A SMOKE?

HEY! IT'S COLONEL TADOKORO!

ONE DAY, I'LL KNOCK HIM FLYING...

HE HIT ME WITH THE RICE BUCKET ONCE.

THAT BASTARD KANEDA'S GOT SOME NERVE, HUH?

MM HMM.

SIR!

YES, SIR. THEY DO LOOK VERY SIMILAR.

YOU MEN, DON'T YOU THINK THE TERRAIN OF BAIEN QUITE RESEMBLES MINATOGAWA*?

*WHERE THE DECISIVE BATTLE BETWEEN THE IMPERIAL FORCES AND THE REBEL ASHIKAGA CLAN WAS FOUGHT.

FISH ARE EASY TO CATCH WHEN THEY'RE KNOCKED UNCONSCIOUS BY A GRENADE.

THIS GUY TOO!

WOW! THIS ONE'S HUGE!

AND HERE TOO!

SHIT!

WHAT'S WRONG?

NAKAMOTO! HANG ON!

HEY!

NAKAMOTO!

LISTEN UP!

NAKAMOTO DIED FISHING TODAY.

NAKAMOTOOOO!

PSSH

ALSO, ENEMY PLANES HAVE RECENTLY BEEN SIGHTED CIRCLING AROUND, SO WE'RE ASSIGNED TO SPOTTING.

ON THE CAPTAIN'S ORDERS, WE WILL NO LONGER BE FISHING WITH GRENADES.

ROOKIES TO THE FRONT!

NO, SIR!

KAYAMA, MARUYAMA, AKASAKI—YOU'RE SPOTTING UNDER CORPORAL YOSHIDA. ANY QUESTIONS?

ANY QUESTIONS?

WHHAAP

TAKE OFF YOUR GLASSES.

MARUYAMA, YOU GRINNIN' OVER THERE?

HMPH.

NO SIR

THUD

OOPH

THWAK

SON OF A BITCH!

I'VE GOT MY EYES ON YOU AT ALL TIMES!

UNDERSTAND, MEN?

IF IT WASN'T FOR THIS WAR, IT'D BE PRETTY PEACEFUL HERE.

OH! A MARTIN*!

*SEE NOTES PAGE 366.

RAT A TAT TAT

FLYING PRETTY LOW.

RAT A TAT TAT

SHIT! IT'S FLYING REALLY LOW!

VROOOOM

RAT A TAT TAT

78

AT THAT MOMENT, KAGEYAMA WAS DONE FOR, WITH NOT A SOUL TO SEE IT.

RRRRR

WELL...THE SCALES WERE GOING THE WRONG WAY, YOU KNOW? THE FISH WOULDN'T COME OUT.

KAYAMA, HEY, WHAT HAPPENED TO NAKAMOTO?

MAYBE THEY THOUGHT WE WERE PIGS OR SOMETHING.

THEY'RE FINALLY GONE.

REALLY? SAME AS ME AND AKASAKI.

WE'RE FROM THE SAME TOWN...SHIPPED OUT TOGETHER, TOO.

LOOK, I DON'T WANNA TALK ABOUT NAKAMOTO.

THAT'S A WEIRD WAY TO DIE, HUH?

WE WERE SEPARATED ON THE SHIP AND AT KOKOPO. THEN BACK TOGETHER AGAIN HERE IN BAIEN.

AND WE ALWAYS GOT THE SAME TRANSFERS.

WE MET ON THE TRAIN ON OUR WAY TO THE REGIMENT.

MEH, SOMETHING GOOD'LL HAPPEN ON THE WAY.

WE PROB'LY ALL GOT THE SAME TICKET TO HELL. HA HA HA.

HMM, YEAH.

PROB'LY DESTINY OR SOMETHING.

LITTLE FINGER

WHAT'S THIS!

C'MON, CARRY IT RIGHT. THE WATER'S SPILLING.

SO YOU'RE WITH ME ON BATH DUTY, HUH?

UH, SIR?

YES, SIR.

LOOKS ALMOST AS IF ONE OF YOUR STARS HAS FALLEN OFF, DOESN'T IT?!

YOU THINK THE ARMY'S A JOKE?!

JUST WHAT DO YOU THINK YOU'RE DOING WITH YOUR STARS LIKE THAT!

WHUMP

YOU'RE REALLY SOMETHING, YOU KNOW THAT?!

DON'T 'YES, SIR' ME!

CHRIST.

HMPH.

I'LL BE MORE CAREFUL IN THE FUTURE, SIR.

YOU SAID IT.

PSSSSH

ONE OF THESE DAYS, I'D LIKE TO GIVE IT BACK TO HIM.

JESUS, YOU'VE GOT A BIG ONE!

HOLY—

OKAY, I'M GETTING IN.

HOLY SHIT!

YOU'RE COVERING WITH BOTH HANDS AND IT'S STILL STICKING OUT BELOW.

N-NO, I DON'T.

FROM WHAT I'VE SEEN, I'D SAY YOU'RE THE BIGGEST IN THE COMPANY.

DON'T SAY THAT.

I HAVEN'T SEEN ANYTHING BIGGER SINCE KOKOPO, FOR SURE.

'ZAT SO?

OKAY.

I'M GOING TO PISS IN THE BATH, SO GO AND GET HIS HIGHNESS.

THAT'S A COURT-MARTIAL.

DON'T SHIT IN THERE.

HEH, SOUNDS GREAT!

SLIRK SLIRK POP

FEELS GOOD TO TAKE A BATH ONCE IN A WHILE.

IF THAT'S THE CASE, THEN ENEMY SPIES ARE DEFINITELY IN THIS LOCATION...

MM HMM.

CAPTAIN, YOUR BATH IS READY, SIR.

IT'S THE ONLY EXPLANATION WE HAVE REGARDING THESE SURPRISE ATTACKS.

THERE IS NO DOUBT.

LIEUTENANT HOMU, BAIEN MILITARY POLICE* SECTION LEADER

*SEE NOTES PAGE 366.

85

RRRRRRRR

RRRRRRR

VROOOOOOM

HUP!

FLIP

IT'S AN AIR RAID!

*JAPAN HAS A COMMUNAL BATHING CULTURE; OFFERS TO WASH BACKS ARE NATURAL AND COMMON.

THANK YOU, SIR.

YOU'RE A GOOD SOLDIER. ONE OF THESE DAYS, I'LL GIVE YOU A COMMEN- DATION.

THIS'LL BE FULL PACKS, MEN. UNDERSTOOD?

SO THE SECOND SECTION WILL GO TO PUT THEM DOWN.

THE ENEMY APPEARS TO BE IN THE MIREM INTERIOR...

LISTEN UP!

ROOKIES TO THE FRONT!!

UNDERSTOOD, SIR

WHAP

WHAAP WHAP

FALL OUT!

TEN MINUTES!

HERE.

YOU GOT ANY CIGARETTES?

YUP.

DEFINITELY WON'T BE ABLE TO SLEEP IN THIS WEATHER, HUH, DOC?

WHAT D'YOU THINK HAPPENS WHEN PEOPLE DIE IN THE FIELD?

DON'T BE STUPID.

MUST BE NICE TO BE A CORPSMAN INSTEAD OF AN ENLISTED MAN.

MOVE OUT!

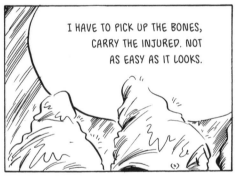

I HAVE TO PICK UP THE BONES, CARRY THE INJURED. NOT AS EASY AS IT LOOKS.

PSSSH

PSSSSHH

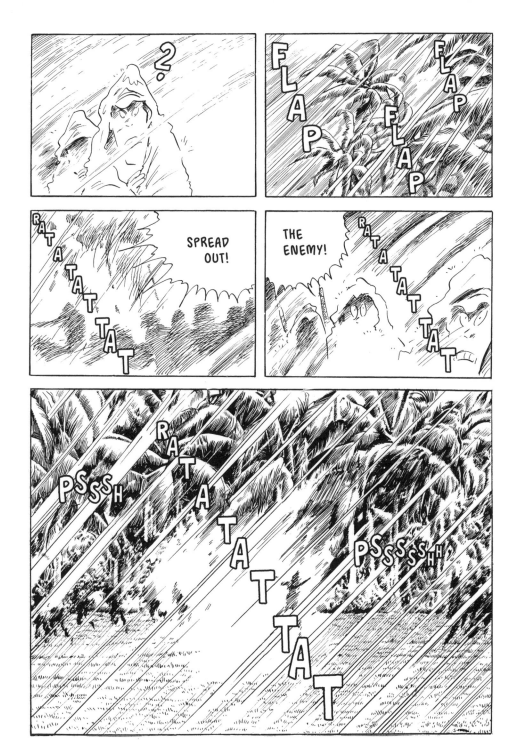

NGGH

AH!

PING

KAYAMA

RAT A TAT ROLL ROLL ROLL

RETREAT!

HUH?

HOLD UP!

PSSSSSSSSH

PSSSSSH

IF WE'RE NOT QUICK, HE'LL FALL INTO ENEMY HANDS.

WHAT DO YOU MEAN?!

I'LL HAVE TO CUT OFF KAYAMA'S FINGER. HELP ME.

PSSSSSSSSH

PSSSSH

I'M STILL ALIVE, GUYS!

RATATATTAT

KAYAMA!

TO PROVE HE DIED IN BATTLE.

WE GOTTA GET HIS LITTLE FINGER OFF QUICK.

TUNK

TUNK

O-O-OKAY.

I'LL HOLD HIM DOWN. YOU TAKE IT OFF WITH THE SHOVEL.

WOULD YOU JUST HURRY UP AND DO IT?

PYOO

IT'S NOT COMIN' OFF.

FOOF

PSSSSSSSSH

PSSSSH

UNH!

ALL BECAUSE THEM SCOUTS AIN'T DOING THEIR JOBS.

WHEN WE ALL CHECKED, SIR...

YES, SIR.

THE ENEMY WAS ON TOP OF THE MOUNTAIN, SIR.

WHAT THE HELL WERE YOU DOING OUT THERE, SCOUT?

SKRITCH SKRITCH

YES, SIR.

YOU'RE IN THE ARMY. IT IS JUST 'WE.' GOT IT?

WHAT'S WITH THIS BUMPKINLY 'WE ALL?'

NOW THEN...

WE'LL SPLIT INTO FOUR GROUPS AND SURROUND THEM.

WE KNOW NOW THAT THE ENEMY IS IN THAT GENERAL DIRECTION.

SHOULD THE FIRST SECTION GO FIRST?

SO IF THAT'S WHAT WE'RE DOING...

THERE CAN'T BE MORE THAN TWENTY OF THEM.

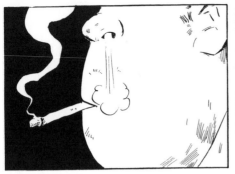

MM HMM. SOUNDS GOOD.

YIPE! THE ENEMY!

POK

RAT A TAT TAT

MACHINE GUNS— FIRE!

RIFLES— FIRE!

RAT A TAT TAT

FIRE!

GET FIRIN' THAT GRENADE LAUNCHER.

READY— ATTACK!

YAAAH

MACHINE-GUN THAT HOUSE!!

THE BASTARDS HAVE RUN OFF.

SILENCE

RAT-A TAT TAT TAT

YUP, THEY'RE GONE.

AND THERE'S CHOCOLATE, TOO!

HOLY SHIT! CANNED FOOD!

THOSE BASTARDS ARE LIVING LIKE KINGS FIGHTING THIS WAR.

WH-WHAT THE HELL...

UH UH!

YOU SAID IT.

YUM!

YOU ASSHOLE!

YOU DON'T GET TREATS LIKE THIS.

ROOKIE LIKE YOU...

WHAAAAAP

WHAT DID YOU SAY?!

I FOUND THE CHOCOLATE FIRST. OPEN YOUR MOUTH, ROOKIE, AND I'LL SEND YOU FLYING.

WHOA, MARUYAMA!

WHAT THE—

HEY! CANNED FOOD!

THAT BASTARD.

GOOD WORK, CORPSMAN.

DOCTOR, THERE WAS ONE DEATH: PRIVATE KAYAMA.

PSSSSH

106

THIS IS KAYAMA'S FINGER. IT'S ALL THAT'S LEFT OF HIM

AND WITH THIS SOUTHERN LOCATION, MORE MEN ARE COMING DOWN WITH FEVERS.

JUST TERRIBLE. POOR MAN.

*MAKI MATCHES

TWO MEN CAN'T EVEN MOVE ANYMORE.

MALARIA?

WE'LL ONLY SEE MORE PATIENTS.

WITH POOR NUTRITION ON TOP OF THE HARD LABOUR...

NEW YEAR'S

SPRING IS A DELIGHT WHEN, ALONE AND DOWN HEARTED, I STAND SENTRY AND WATCH

GIRLS ON THEIR WAY HOME FROM HANAMI* PARTIES

*SEE NOTES PAGE 366.

HEE HEE HEE HEE

HO HO HO HO

YOU BEST REMEMBER YOURSELF.

SIR, I APOLOGIZE.

GETTIN' A BIT CARRIED AWAY, AREN'T YOU?

BOINK

NOT YET.

UH...

YOU WASHED THE SERGEANT'S UNIFORM?

YES, SIR.

IT'S JUST YOU WHO HASN'T.

ALL YOU ROOKIES GOTTA DO IT!

COME ON!

UH, YES.

YOU DO WANNA DO IT, RIGHT?

YOU BETTER.

I'LL DO IT RIGHT AWAY.

SKRTCH SKRTCH

OH, THAT'D BE GOOD.

MY LAUNDRY!?

HMM?

SERGEANT, PLEASE LET ME WASH YOUR UNIFORM!

SKRTCH SKRTCH

CHRIST. HIS SKIVVIES, TOO?

YES, SIR.

WHILE YOU'RE AT IT, CAN YOU DO MY SKIVVIES, TOO?

HEY! I STILL HAVE A BUNCH MORE HERE.

DAMMIT! THERE'S SHIT STUCK TO THESE.

SUPPOSED TO BE A DAY OFF AND HERE I AM...

SPLISH SPLISH

SQUAAWK AAWK

PLOSH

ALL NCOS AND OFFICERS, ASSEMBLE!

GODDAMNED PARROT.

PFFT

YES, SIR?

HEY, MARUYAMA!

YES, SIR.

BRING THE SERGEANT HIS SUPPER.

THERE'S A PARTY FOR THE OFFICERS AND THE NCOS.

WHY AM I THE ONLY ONE BEING WORKED LIKE A SLAVE ON NEW YEAR'S?

*SEE NOTES ON PAGE 366.

mmm.

HOW ABOUT IT, CAPTAIN? YOU NEXT?

CLAP CLAP CLAP

THE CAPTAIN'S SINGING CRAP LIKE THIS?

CLAP

CLAP

CLAP

HERE YOU ARE, SIR.

HEY! SUPPER!

LISTEN UP!

YES, SIR!

TOMORROW, KIRIMOTO, MARUYAMA, TANAKA, YOU'RE GATHERING VEGETABLES.

WHAT THE— IT'S NEW YEAR'S!

ROOKIES TO THE FRONT!

WHAP

WHAAAP

HEY, WHAT'S THAT?

IT'S A TORPEDO BOAT.

LOOKS LIKE A SHIP.

RAT-A-TAT TAT TAT

RAT A TAT TAT TAT

WHAT THE HELL WAS THAT?!

THEM ENEMY SOLDIERS'LL BE COMING ASHORE PRETTY SOON!

I HEARD THEY SNEAK IN AT NIGHT AND CHECK HOW DEEP THE WATER IS.

HEY, YOU WANNA TAKE THAT PAPAYA OVER THERE BACK WITH US?

THE ROOTS?

YOU CAN EAT PAPAYA ROOTS, YOU KNOW.

WE DO ONLY GET TWO SLICES A DAY, AND PICKLED TO BOOT.

THEN LET'S TAKE THE ROOTS TOO.

YEAH. TASTES LIKE A CROSS BETWEEN DAIKON RADISH AND BURDOCK*.

*SEE NOTES PAGE 367.

PULL A
LITTLE
HARDER.

VROOOOM

*SEE NOTES PAGE 367.

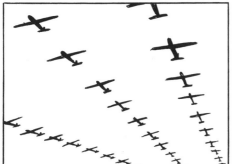

YOU SAID IT...

THEY'LL BE BACK SOON ENOUGH.

THEY'RE FINALLY GONE.

GET OUT THERE AND HELP FIND HIM.

...

HAPPY TO SEE A VET DEAD— WHAT KIND OF ASSHOLES ARE YOU?

SPLOSH

SPLASH

THIRD DAY OF THIS CRAP.

YOU'RE PROB'LY RIGHT.

THE CORPORAL'S DEFINITELY IN SOME GATOR'S STOMACH, GETTING DIGESTED AND TURNED INTO CRAP RIGHT NOW.

BUT THE MEN HAVE BEEN SEARCHING FOR THREE DAYS NOW. ISN'T IT ABOUT TIME TO LET IT GO?

NOGAMI WAS A GOOD MAN. THE LEAST WE CAN DO IS FIND HIS BODY. HIS SPIRIT WILL BE STUCK IF WE DON'T.

NOGAMI WON'T BE ABLE TO REST OTHERWISE.

EVEN IF IT'S JUST A LEG, JUST AN ARM, WE HAVE TO FIND SOMETHING OF HIM!

DON'T SAY THAT, SIR!

... THE CAMP IS THE CAMP; THIS IS ABOUT HUMAN DIGNITY.

BUT WHAT ABOUT THE CAMP CONSTRUCTION?

HMM... WELL, THIS IS A PROBLEM.

NO MATTER WHAT, I HAVE TO HELP NOGAMI REST IN PEACE.

THREE DAYS PASSED AND THEN FOUR, AND STILL THE BODY OF CORPORAL NOGAMI WAS NOWHERE TO BE FOUND.

SIR, IF WE HAVEN'T FOUND HIM THIS FAR UP THE RIVER, HE'S NOT HERE.

HA HA HA HA!

TO FOOL AROUND.

HE'S USING IT AS AN EXCUSE...

SERGEANT HONDA'S REALLY STUCK ON THIS SEARCH.

WE SURE HAVE IT EASY NOW.

THINKING BACK TO OUR DAYS AT THE CAMP...

IT'S BEEN ALMOST A WEEK.

LIEUTENANT HOMU!

MIZUMOTO, YOU WANT TO PLAY MAHJONG?

WE'RE SHORT ONE MAN.

PERFECT. THEN COME ALONG TO THE POLICE HQ.

I'D BE DELIGHTED TO JOIN YOU, SIR.

I WOULD NEVER HAVE THOUGHT I WOULD END UP PLAYING MAHJONG AT THE FRONT.

WE ALL KNEW YOU WERE HIDING SOMETHING.

UH, YES.

YOU'RE SHOOTING FOR THE RED DRAGON, AREN'T YOU?

HERE.

HESITATING WILL GET YOU KILLED IN THIS PLACE.

YOU GONNA TAKE IT? YOU NEED IT, DON'T YOU?

LETTING YOUR SOLDIERS FOOL AROUND FOR A WHOLE WEEK.

!! ?

TO HAVE FORTY SOLDIERS DIGGING AROUND BECAUSE A SINGLE COLONEL DIED IS JUST DAMNED RIDICULOUS.

THOSE SOLDIERS DON'T BELONG TO YOU.

HOW ABOUT YOU QUIT FOOLING AROUND WITH THIS CORPSE BUSINESS?

THANK YOU, SIR.

I'LL LET IT GO THIS TIME.

YES, SIR.

SO THEY'RE WATCHING ME...

THE ENEMY ARRIVES

THE ENEMY TURNED
THE CAMP ON THE
MOUNTAIN INTO
A WASTELAND.

OFFICERS, ASSEMBLE AT HQ!

A GROUP OF ENEMY TRANSPORT SHIPS IS HEADED THIS WAY.

ACCORDING TO THE REPORTS WE'VE JUST RECEIVED...

IT'S BEEN DECIDED THAT WE WILL BE DEPLOYED FOR COMBAT.

AFTER DISCUSSION WITH LIEUTENANT -COLONEL TADOKORO...

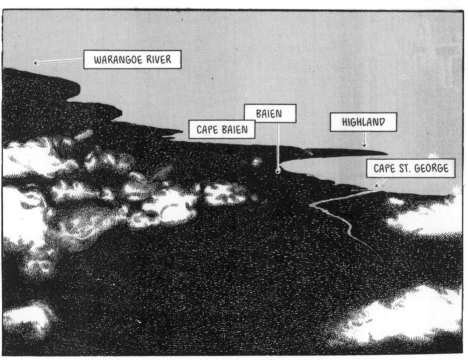

THUD

HUP!

YES, SIR.

THREE GRENADES EACH.

ONCE YOU GOT 'EM, GET INTO POSITION.

WHAT'RE YOU DAWDLING FOR?!

I NEED TO TAKE A SHIT.

HURRY UP THEN.

I NEED TO TAKE A LEAK.

IDIOTS! JUST GET IN THE DAMNED HOLE!

ARE THEY COMING OR NOT?

THEY'RE HERE!

143

KKKABOOM

OKAY!

FIRE THE CANNON!

AND HERE WE GO.

INCOMING!

VROOOOM

RAT A TAT TAT TAT

B**OOM**

WAS IT BRAVE
TO FIRE? RECKLESS?
SILENCE REIGNED AFTER
THE BATTALION'S SINGLE
CANNON SHOT.

149

GUYS, THEY SENT KONISHI FLYING!

TAKING A LEAK.

WHAT WAS KONISHI DOING, SIR?

KADUNK THUNK

TAT TAT TAT

I'M THINKING THEY SET UP GUNS AT THE MOUTH OF THE WARANGOE.

NO, IT'S NOT THAT.

THE SHIP'S GUNS?

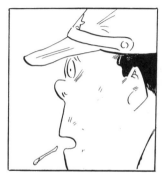

DID THEY?

AH!

WHAT?!

THERE'S A HUGE SHIP COMING RIGHT AT US!

THERE IT IS!

KRRR

KRRR

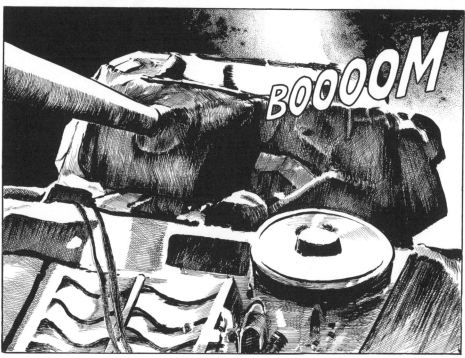

SPECIAL ATTACK UNIT

LIEUTENANT-COLONEL TADOKORO!

THE ENEMY.

WHAT IS IT, CAPTAIN?

THEY HAVE A TANK HEADED STRAIGHT FOR MY COMPANY.

THEY STORMED THE BEACHHEAD AND TOOK THE WARANGOE.

BOTH THE COMPANY CAMP AND THE WARANGOE CAMP HAVE BEEN DESTROYED.

EXACTLY AS PLANNED...

I UNDERSTAND, CAPTAIN. WE HAVE ONLY OUR HUMAN BODIES TO THROW AGAINST ENEMY MATERIEL!

WE'RE DOWN TO JUST TWO COMPANIES, SIR.

AND WE WILL ATTACK THE ENEMY'S BEACH-HEAD POSITION TONIGHT!

WE WILL IMMEDIATELY FORM A SPECIAL ATTACK UNIT...

BUT THE GREAT MASTER KUSUNOKI* HAD ONLY FIVE HUNDRED AGAINST THOUSANDS, DID HE NOT?

I KNOW!

BUT, SIR, THE ENEMY FORCES ARE...

*SEE NOTES FOR PAGE 29 IN NOTES SECTION PAGE 366.

IF WE FIGHT WITH EVERY OUNCE OF OUR STRENGTH, WE WILL BE ABLE TO HOLD FOR A FEW DAYS.

WHEN WE REMEMBER MASTER KUSUNOKI, THIS IS NOTHING.

DO NOT SPEAK TO ME OF RETREAT!

MOVE TO HIGHER GROUND AND ENGAGE IN GUERILLA TACTICS, WE CAN HOLD FOR A YEAR, MAYBE TWO.

IF WE RETREAT TEMPORARILY...

A FEW DAYS?

BAM BAM BAM BAM

FOOLISHNESS!

WHAT?! OUR HEAVY ARTILLERY HAS BEEN DESTROYED?!

SIR, I HAVE A MESSAGE!

162

PUT TOGETHER AN ATTACK UNIT TO TAKE OUT THE TANKS...

YES, SIR.

I SEE— LIEUTENANT!

TAKE TWO OR THREE MEN FROM EACH SQUAD AND PUT TOGETHER A SPECIAL ATTACK UNIT.

YES, SIR.

AT THE ENEMY'S BEACHHEAD BASE.

CARRY THE ATTACKS OUT TONIGHT.

THIS IS THE ONLY PATH LEFT FOR US.

TWO MEN FROM EACH SECTION COME AND GET IT!

HEY! WE'RE GIVING OUT THE LAST OF THE GRUB!

YES, SIR.

AND NO DILLY-DALLYING!

ROOKIES, YOU GO!

I'M PRETTY SICK OF IT.

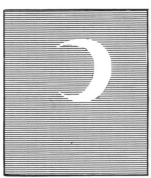

YOU SAID IT.

IT'S BEEN OVER A YEAR AND STILL, IT'S 'ROOKIES THIS,' 'ROOKIES THAT.' RIGHT, AKASAKI?

YES, SIR.

TAKE THE RICE BACK TO YOUR SQUADS.

ONE MAN, ONE BAG.

KREEE

KREEE

I DON'T KNOW WHEN THE NEXT SUPPLY DROP WILL BE.

SO MAKE THIS LAST.

IT'S TOO QUIET.

I CAN'T GO ANY FARTHER.

REALLY?

SEEMS LIKE JUST ONE REGIMENT CAME ASHORE.

LET'S TAKE A BREAK.

OH YEAH.

REMEMBER HOW WE MET BEFORE WE EVEN JOINED UP?

KLAKETTA

KLAKETTA

I THOUGHT SO.

YES, I AM.

UM, EXCUSE ME—ARE YOU ALSO JOINING UP?

IN—IN THAT BOMB HOLE.

YOU REALLY MOVE WHEN BANANAS ARE INVOLVED.

YEAH, KEEP SOME OTHER SECTION FROM EATING THEM.

COVER IT WITH SOME LEAVES.

WELL, I HEARD THAT A SINGLE BANANA CAN GIVE YOU ENOUGH CALORIES TO WORK A WHOLE DAY.

HQ'S NEAR DESTRUCTION

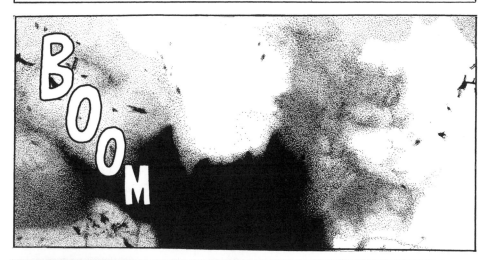

I'M PART OF TONIGHT'S SPECIAL ATTACK UNIT.

BUT, SIR...

HEY, YOU! GO GET SOME WATER!

IDIOT!

BUT IT'S RAINING BOMBS...

WHEN I TELL YOU TO GO, YOU GO!

I'LL GO AND FETCH THE WATER, SIR.

WHAAAP

WE'RE IN THE MIDDLE OF A WAR. DON'T QUIBBLE WITH ME!

THIS SUCKS EGGS.

175

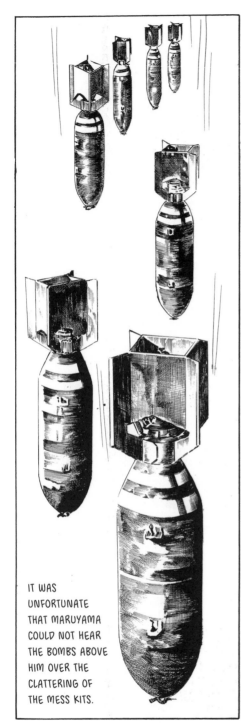

IT WAS UNFORTUNATE THAT MARUYAMA COULD NOT HEAR THE BOMBS ABOVE HIM OVER THE CLATTERING OF THE MESS KITS.

JUST ANOTHER ASSHOLE WHO THINKS I'M A WORM.

CLATTER CLATTER CLATTER

PYOOO

AAAH!

176

JUST AWFUL.

WOW!

GOT HIMSELF DECORATED.

WITH HIS SPECIAL ATTACK UNIT, MIURA DID SOME REAL DAMAGE TO THOSE BASTARDS.

THE S.O.B. TOOK ALL OUR MESS KITS— HE'S PROB'LY HAVING A SNACK!

THAT MARUYAMA SURE IS TAKING HIS TIME!

HMM, STRANGE.

?

RAT A TAT TAT TAT TAT TAT

178

I'LL CHECK IT OUT.

IT SOUNDS VERY CLOSE...

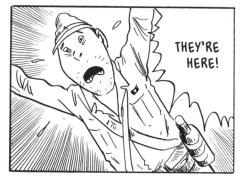

THEY'RE HERE!

SHI—

CHAK

MACHINE GUNS, FIRE!

RAT A TAT TAT

TAT TAT TAT

CAN YOU GET IT WORKING? THEY'RE COMING!

IT'S JAMMED!

YES, SIR.

BANG BAM

WHAT ABOUT THE GUN?!

FFFT

CHAK CHAK

STILL JAMMED!

BAM BAM BAM BAM BAM

AH!

FLOP

THE SHOT KILLED CORPORAL YOSHIDA, THE SECTION LEADER, AND PRIVATE AKASAKI.

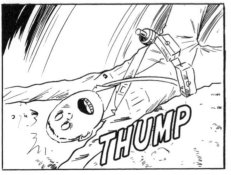

THUMP

TWITCH TWITCH

SINCE THEY COULDN'T FLEE THEIR POSITION...

DAMMIT!

TWO OR THREE MEN SURVIVED, BUT...

THEY FOUGHT UNTIL THE END; EIGHT SOLDIERS OF THE FIRST SECTION WERE ANNIHILATED.

UHH...

WHAT'RE YOU DOING OVER HERE? THE ENEMY'S COMING.

THE SURVIVOR KIRIMOTO CAME ACROSS MARUYAMA, WHO HAD LOST CONSCIOUS-NESS AFTER THE BLAST.

188

SERGEANT, IT'S THE ENEMY.

IT'S SERGEANT HONDA!

HUF
HUF

HUF

CORPORAL YOSHIDA'S SECTION'S BEEN WIPED OUT.

SERGEANT HONDA!

WHY THE HELL'D YOU RETREAT?!

THERE'S A MEDIC THAT WAY. GO!

SO THAT AREA'S FALLEN INTO ENEMY HANDS?

WHAT'S WRONG WITH YOU?

CORPSMAN KAMIYA!

HEY! DOC'S OVER HERE!

I GOT HIT IN A BOMB BLAST AND NOW I'M ALL DIZZY.

YES, SIR.

I TOLD YOU TO HELP, SO HELP!

BUT, I—

YOU'RE FINE! GIVE HIM A HAND.

HERE! HOLD THIS FOR ME.

IT'S OUT OF CONTROL.

WE HAVE THIS MANY CASUALTIES AND MALARIA VICTIMS?

THERE'S A HOLE OUTSIDE THE CAMP.

YES, SIR.

TOSS

HOLD HIM DOWN.

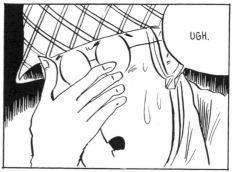

UGH.

CAN YOU HELP A MAN THIS FAR GONE, DOCTOR?

MY JOB IS TO EXTEND THE LIVES OF THESE MEN, EVEN IF IT'S JUST FOR A FEW SECONDS.

I'M A DOCTOR.

...YES, SIR.

AAAGH

IT HURTS
IT HURTS

OUT OF
THE WAY!

GET IN
LINE!

VROOOOM

THEY'RE HERE!

BAM

BAM BAM

BAM

BLAM

THE CORPSMAN ASKED ME TO HELP, SO—

SIR!

MARUYAMA, WHAT THE HELL'RE YOU DOIN'?

HURRY UP AND FIRE!

IDIOT!

WHAAAAP

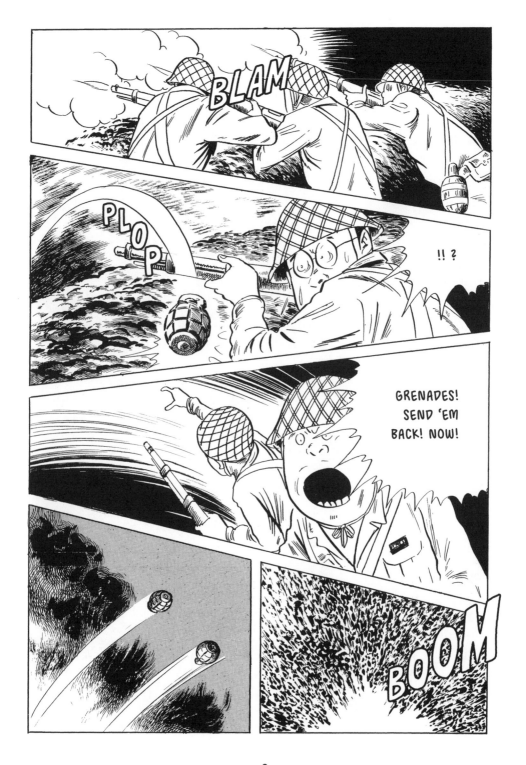

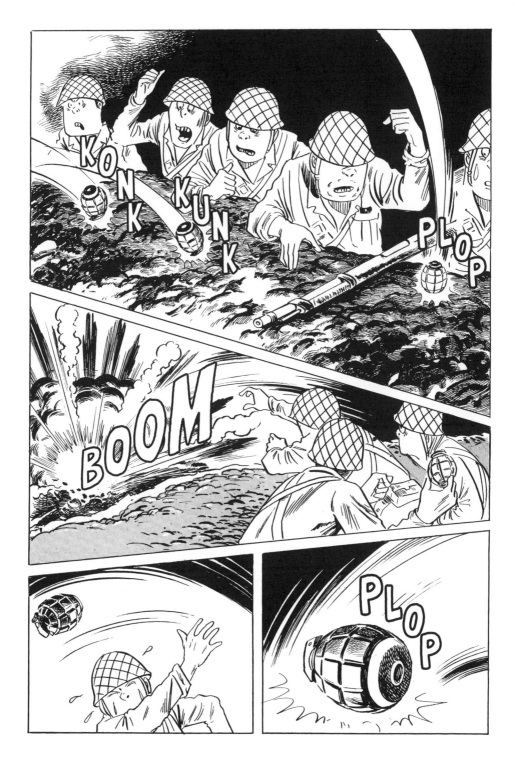

SERGEANT HONDA!

THE SITUATION'S COMPLETELY CHANGED. THE ENEMY HAS TAKEN THE RIVER.

WHAT?!

THE ORDER'S COME TO RETREAT TO BATTALION HQ!

MEN! FALL BACK!

THAT IS BAD.

THE RIVER?

GRIN

MIURA! LOOK OUT!

BLAM

GET THE HELL OUT OF HERE! THOSE BASTARDS ARE COMIN'!

SHI—MIURA...

THE DEATH OF SERGEANT HONDA

THE ONLY OPTION LEFT AT THIS POINT IS A NOBLE DEATH*.

THE ENEMY WENT AROUND AND TOOK THE RIVER FROM THE REAR; THEY HAVE NOW SURROUNDED US.

*SEE NOTES PAGE 367.

WE'LL CHARGE THE ENEMY TOGETHER.

LIKE MASTER KUSUNOKI BEFORE US...

DEATH!!

TO CHARGE THEM EXPECTING ONLY ANNIHILATION— IT'S UNTHINKABLE.

BUT SIR, WE CANNOT POSSIBLY TRIUMPH OVER THEIR FORCES.

BY PROTECTING RABAUL FOR ONE DAY, EVEN TWO DAYS?

ALSO PROTECT OUR MOTHER-LAND...

DO WE NOT...

IT'S ABSOLUTE LUNACY.

YOU MEAN RETREAT BEHIND THE MOUNTAIN AND ENGAGE IN GUERILLA TACTICS?

ONE DAY, TWO DAYS— WE CAN COVER RABAUL FOR A MONTH OR EVEN SIX.

WE WILL NOT BE ABLE TO MUSTER UP THE ENERGY AND COURAGE TO CONFRONT SUCH SUPERIOR NUMBERS.

THE MOMENT WE LEAVE THIS CAMP...

THE SOLDIERS WILL JUST STARVE OR FALL VICTIM TO MALARIA.

LIVING IN THE JUNGLE FOR A WEEK, A MONTH...

IT IS MUCH NOBLER FOR ALL OF US TO DIE IN A SUICIDE CHARGE NOW.

FAR BETTER THAN THAT TRAGIC DEATH IS TO ATTACK NOW WHILE WE HAVE THE STRENGTH.

CAPTAIN, ARE YOU SAYING THAT YOU WILL NOT DIE ALONGSIDE ME?!

SIR, EVEN IF WE DO CARRY OUT A SUICIDE CHARGE, IT'S NOT CLEAR HOW MUCH DAMAGE WE CAN INFLICT ON THE ENEMY.

SIR, BEHIND US AT RABAUL, A HUNDRED THOUSAND SOLDIERS ARE JUST LOUNGING AROUND RIGHT NOW.

WE MUST DIE ON THIS GODFORSAKEN ISLAND.

WE, ON THE OTHER HAND, HAVE HARDLY ANYTHING TO EAT AND...

WATCH YOUR TONGUE, CAPTAIN!

IS PROTECTING THIS LITTLE PLATEAU SO GODDAMNED IMPORTANT? SUCH LENGTHS TO HOLD THIS PLACE...IT'S A GODDAMNED FARCE!

YOU WILL CLOSE YOUR MOUTH AND JOIN ME IN DEATH.

THE GENERAL OF THE IMPERIAL ARMY ORDERED US TO HOLD THIS PLATEAU!

TO SACRIFICE OURSELVES TO PROLONG THE LIVES OF THOSE HUNDRED THOUSAND SOLDIERS IN RABAUL...

SIR, AT THE RISK OF REPEATING MYSELF, IF OUR AIM IS...

WE COULD BEST ACHIEVE THIS BY RETREATING BEHIND THE MOUNTAIN AND ENGAGING IN GUERILLA TACTICS.

AS COMMANDER OF THESE FORCES, I CANNOT ORDER MY MEN TO DIE LIKE DOGS!

THAT'S ONLY IF IT GOES WELL AND IN THE END, WE WILL ONLY BE MAKING OUR MEN DIE LIKE DOGS.

HOW DARE YOU?!

A SUICIDE CHARGE IS THE DOG'S DEATH!

LIKE DOGS...

YOU FOOL!

I WILL NOT DIE WITH YOU!

YOU HAVE NO CHOICE. I HAVE ORDERED THE SUICIDE CHARGE!

IT'S VERY DOUBTFUL THE MEN OF THIS BATTALION WILL ACCEPT AN ORDER FOR AN IMMEDIATE SUICIDE CHARGE.

BUT...

LIEUTENANT-COLONEL, SIR, I UNDERSTAND YOUR POSITION.

WAITING TWO OR THREE DAYS TO CONSIDER ALL THE ANGLES WOULD BE BEST.

HMM.

PERHAPS IT WOULD BE BETTER TO DEFER THIS FOR THE MOMENT, SIR?

SIGH

GOT IT!

CUT THE VINES ON THE TREES AND HAVE A DRINK. WATER DRIPS OUT, YOU KNOW.

HUH.

I'M SO THIRSTY I CAN'T THINK.

CRAP, THEY'RE ALREADY CUT.

SHFF SHFF

ALL RIGHT!

GOTTA GO SOME-
WHERE THE GUYS
HAVEN'T ALREADY
GOT TO.

VSH

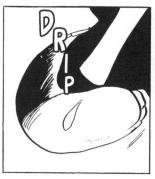

DRIP

GULP

DRIP

BAM
BAM
BAM

SHF
SHF

HEH

WHO WAS THAT?

AGH

BE CAREFUL, GUYS.

THEY MUST BE.

GUESS THE ENEMY'S CLOSE THEN.

KOJIMA.

THE BASTARDS GOT HIM?

SERGEANT HONDA, KOJIMA IS—

GOTTA TELL THE SARGE.

I'LL GO TAKE A LOOK.

WONDER IF THE ENEMY'S GOTTEN CLOSER.

STRANGE.

YES, SIR.

YOU, COME WITH ME.

SHFF SHFF

IT'S THEM!

SHFF SHFF

SHFF SHFF

THE ENEMY!

AHH

BLAM

AUGH! GIMME YOUR GRENADE!

SERGEANT HONDA!

THAK

BOOM

GET BACK!

 WE'VE GOT SOME MEN LOOKING FOR ANOTHER SOURCE OF WATER.

 I KNOW THAT!

SIR, WE CAN'T COOK THE RICE WITHOUT ANY WATER.

 WE'LL DEAL WITH THE BODIES OF SERGEANT HONDA AND KOJIMA TOMORROW.

 IN ANY CASE, NO ONE LEAVES THIS TRENCH TONIGHT.

 SIR, WHAT'S GOING TO HAPPEN NOW?

 KEEP YOUR GUNS LOADED AND AT HAND.

WE'LL SET SENTRIES BEFORE WE SLEEP.

 ALL I DREAM ABOUT IS STEAK.

 MM HMM.

EVERY NIGHT, I JUST DREAM OF FOOD.

SIR, I HEARD THEY'RE BOMBING JAPAN EVERY DAY NOW.

IF WE KEEP EATING UNCOOKED RICE, WE'RE GOING TO HAVE MANY MORE MEN GET SICK FROM MALARIA.

WHAT'RE WE DOING FIGHTING A WAR HERE?

IF EVERYTHING AT HOME IS CRAZY LIKE THAT—

MM HMM.

JUST GO TO SLEEP AND DREAM ABOUT EATING SUSHI OR SOMETHING.

I HAVE NO IDEA.

FORGET ABOUT THAT. I'M HAVING SUKIYAKI!

YOU COULD HAVE SOME TEA WITH IT!

SUSHI!

NOW THAT YOU MENTION IT...

SO YOU LIKE YOKAN*?

NAH, WHAT I REALLY MISS IS THE TASTE OF ANPAN*!

HOW 'BOUT YOU? SAKE?

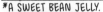
*A SWEET BEAN JELLY.

*BUN FILLED WITH A SWEET BEAN PASTE.

WHEN I WAS IN CHINA, I SLEPT WITH A SPANISH GIRL.

FOOD'S FINE AN' DANDY, BUT WHAT I WOULDN'T GIVE FOR A WOMAN.

IT'S BEEN AT LEAST THREE YEARS SINCE I HAD THAT TREAT.

I FORGET HER NAME.

WAS IT CARMEN?

A SPANISH GIRL?!

IT WAS... AMAZING.

HEY!

BUT JAPANESE GIRLS ARE THE BEST!

YOU GUYS CAN SAY WHATEVER YOU WANT...

THE RUSSIANS ARE GOOD, TOO. WHEN I WAS IN HARBIN*...

*SEE NOTES PAGE 367.

AND I MAY BE A VIRGIN, BUT BULLSHIT LIKE THIS—

I HAVE A HUNDRED-AND-FOUR-DEGREE FEVER.

UH HUH.

DON'T YOU HAVE MALARIA?

WHAT'RE WE GONNA DO ABOUT WATER TOMORROW?

CHRIST, I'M THIRSTY.

YOU REALLY DO.

I GET A LITTLE EXCITED!

BLAM

BLAM

BLAM

BLAM

WHAT'S WRONG WITH YOU?

MUST BE 'CAUSE THE ATTACK IS DOING THEIR SUICIDE CHARGE.

LISTEN TO THAT. THE ENEMY'S GOING NUTS OUT THERE.

DO SOME-THIN' TO COOL ME DOWN.

CAN'T TELL THE DIFFERENCE BETWEEN DAY AND NIGHT NO MORE.

CAUGHT SOMETHIN' ON ACCOUNT OF BEING STUCK HERE WHILE THEY BOMB AND SHOOT.

FEVER.

OH, RIGHT. YOU'RE THE ONE WHO KILLED THE SERGEANT!

SERGEANT HONDA AND THEN SEVEN OTHER GUYS...

WHAT ABOUT THE GUYS FROM YOUR SECTION?

C'MON, I SAID SHUT UP ABOUT IT.

EVEN A TOUGH GUY LIKE HIM'S NO MATCH FOR A BULLET.

DON'T REMIND ME!

PROB'LY 'CAUSE THE FIRST PLATOON RETREATED TOO SOON, AND WITHOUT ORDERS.

WIPED OUT WITH THE CAMP, I GUESS.

WHAT ABOUT YOUR SECTION?

WITH SWEET TEA! KAPPOREE*! WITH BITTER TEA! KAPPOREE!

*SEE NOTES PAGE 367.

NOW THAT YOU MENTION IT, THINGS DID CHANGE PRETTY QUICK.

HA HA HA HA

IT'S UCHIDA!

WHO'S THAT?!

HA HA HA HA

S-STOP HIM! HE'S HEADED FOR THE ENEMY!

HOLY SHIT, HE'S TOUGH.

WHAT THE HELL'RE YOU DOIN'?

HA HA HA HA!

UCHIDA!

HOLD ON TO HIM!

TIE HIM TO A TREE.

HE'S REALLY SWINGING...

RESTRAIN HIM!

BOOM

ASKED ABOUT THE YAMATO SPIRIT OF SHIKISHIMA*

THE FRAGRANCE OF THE MOUNTAIN CHERRY BLOSSOM IN THE MORNING SUN

*SEE NOTES PAGE 367.

KREE
KREE

YOU KNOW, LIEUTENANT, THE ANCIENTS WERE RIGHT WHEN THEY SAID THERE IS A TIME WHEN EVERY SOLDIER MUST FACE HIS DEATH.

I DON'T BELIEVE THAT IS THE CASE, SIR.

FIGHTING WITH GUERILLA TACTICS AND PROLONGING OUR LIVES...THIS WILL ONLY BRING US SHAME.

IT'S THE DECISION TO FACE IT THAT'S IMPORTANT.

BUT, SIR...THE SOLDIERS OF THIS BATTALION ARE NOT PREPARED FOR A SUICIDE MISSION.

GUERILLA WARFARE WILL BE MORE DIFFICULT THAN A SUICIDE CHARGE, WILL IT NOT?

IN THE JUNGLE, WITH NO FOOD AVAILABLE TO US...

BUT I'D LIKE TO DETERMINE THE PLACE OF MY DEATH.

I MAY BE MERELY A CAREER SOLDIER...

A SUICIDE CHARGE IS OUR ONLY OPTION!

SO YOU'RE SAYING—

SOLDIERS! ASSEMBLE FOR BRIEFING!

I'M DONE FOR.

HAAH

JESUS, YOU'RE BURNING UP.

WHAT?!

HEY, ANPAN!

HA HA HA

KOBAYASHI!

I'VE ENDED UP LIKE THAT ONCE OR TWICE.

OKAY.

HIS BRAIN'S COOKED. LET HIM SLEEP.

YOU KNOW, ANPAN.

GUYS— LISTEN UP!

OH YEAH?

HAPPENS TO JUST ABOUT EVERYONE ONCE THE FEVER GETS OVER FORTY-TWO OR SO.

SILENCE

AT ONE O'CLOCK IN THE MORNING...

THE WOUNDED AND THE MEN WITH MALARIA...

YOU'LL FOLLOW THE DOCTOR'S INSTRUCTIONS. THE REST WILL JOIN US AND FIGHT.

EACH PLATOON WILL MAKE A FINAL AND DECISIVE BANZAI CHARGE ON THE ENEMIES SURROUNDING US.

SILENCE

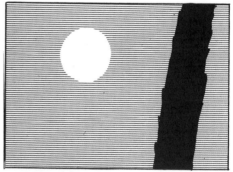

A SUICIDE CHARGE?

THE SAKE BEING DISTRIBUTED NOW IS THE LAST OF IT.

I'LL HELP YOU.

WHY SHOULD I?

KOBAYASHI, GET OVER TO THE DOCTOR.

I'LL HELP YOU, MARUYAMA.

THOSE WHO ARE SERIOUSLY WOUNDED, USE YOUR GRENADES.

THE ORDER FOR A SUICIDE CHARGE HAS BEEN GIVEN.

YOU'LL GO IN WITH ME.

ONCE THE PLATOONS HAVE ATTACKED...

YOU OTHER WOUNDED MEN...

ONES THAT CAN'T, WELL, THEY HAVE THEIR GRENADES.

ANYONE WHO CAN MOVE GOES.

DOCTOR, WHAT ABOUT THE MEN WITH FEVERS?

SECOND PLATOON! FALL IN!

MMM.

KOBAYASHI, HOW'RE YOU DOING?

OH? WHERE?

I GOTTA GO, KOBAYASHI.

229

...

MOOSH

KREE
KREE

CORPORAL KAWAKITA! IS THAT YOU?

AAAAAH.

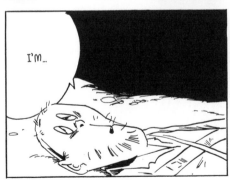

I'M...

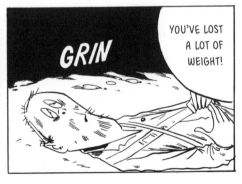

GRIN

YOU'VE LOST A LOT OF WEIGHT!

I CAN'T
MOVE...

I KNOW
WHAT YOU
WANT.

DO ME A
FAVOUR?

IF YOU EVER
GET OUT BY
MATSUSAKA*...

*A CITY IN MIE PREFECTURE IN SOUTHWEST HONSHU.

SECOND PLATOON!
ALL SOLDIERS
FALL IN!

I'M AN
ONLY
CHILD.

YOUR MOTHER
LIVES ALONE IN
MATSU-
SAKA...

ALL THE GUYS I KNOW,
THEY'RE JUST DYING
ONE RIGHT AFTER
THE OTHER.

GOODBYE,
SIR.

NOBLE DEATH

HA HA HA!

DRINK UP!

YEAH, "I'M A BLOSSOM THAT FALLS IN THE RED-LIGHT DISTRICT!"

"WILTING IN THE DAY, BLOOMING AT NIGHT," HUH? HA HA!

WILTING IN THE DAY BLOOMING AT NIGHT

TO THE RIGHT! RIGHT!

LET US TURN NOW TOWARDS OUR BELOVED HOMELAND AND BOW IN FAREWELL.

I MYSELF WILL ATTACK FROM THE CENTER TOGETHER WITH THE SECOND COMPANY AND THE FIRST PLATOON.

EACH PLATOON WILL ADVANCE IN THE DIRECTION ORDERED.

FIX BAYON—ETS!

MOVE OUT!

PERHAPS MAJOR TADOKORO,
WHO HAD LIVED HIS LIFE LONGING FOR A
GLORIOUS DEATH, FORGOT ABOUT THE MEN
UNDER HIM. HE DISAPPEARED QUICKLY INTO
THE DEEP DARKNESS, HIS MEN SOON LOSING
SIGHT OF HIM. BUT HE WAS DEFINITELY
LEADING THE CHARGE.

AROUND THE TIME THE DEEP NIGHT
FINALLY SLIPPED OFF IN THE LIGHT,
THE CAPTAIN, UNABLE TO MOVE WITH
THE WOUND TO HIS LEG, WAS HELPED
BY HIS SOLDIERS IN THE DIRECTION OF
CAPE ST. GEORGE FROM THE BACKSIDE
OF THE MOUNTAIN. HE SHOULD NOT
HAVE STILL BEEN ALIVE.

BUT THE CAPTAIN
WAS ALIVE.

THANK YOU,
SIR.

GOOD
JOB,
MEN.

PUT YOU DOWN, SIR?
INJURED LIKE THIS IN
THE MIDDLE OF
NOWHERE?

THIS IS FAR
ENOUGH. PUT
ME DOWN.

HE BREATHED SLOWLY AS IF TO REFLECT UPON EACH MINUTE, EACH SECOND.

CAPTAIN, LET US TAKE YOU WITH US TO CAPE ST. GEORGE

WHEN I TELL YOU TO PUT ME DOWN, YOU PUT ME DOWN.

WE WERE ORDERED ON A SUICIDE CHARGE. HOW COULD YOUR CAPTAIN HAVE THE AUDACITY TO SHOW HIS FACE ALIVE?

DON'T BE FOOLISH. I CAN'T GO WITH YOU.

YOU MEN ARE FINE AS YOU ARE. YOU'RE RETREATING ON MY ORDERS.

UH, WELL... THEN WE—

IT'S IMPOS-SIBLE. PUT ME DOWN.

CAPTAIN, SIR, COME WITH US...

THIS IS THE PLACE WHERE MY LIFE WILL END.

YES, SIR.

THAT'S AN ORDER!

LEAVE ME AND GO.

CAPE ST. GEORGE IS THIS WAY.

SIR, DON'T TALK LIKE THAT!

AND THAT THE WAR WILL SOON BE DECIDED.

WE'VE HEARD OUR HOMELAND IS ALSO BEING BOMBED...

SIR...

BUT THIS IS AN ORDER.

THANK YOU, PRIVATE.

MAYBE THE SITUATION HAS CHANGED.

CAPTAIN!!

LEAVE ME AND GO.

TELL MY FAMILY THAT I LEFT THIS EARTH ON MARCH 18TH*.

IF YOU MEN SOMEHOW LIVE AND RETURN HOME...

*SEE NOTES PAGE 367.

245

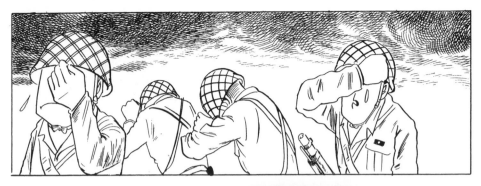

WHEN I TELL YOU TO GO, YOU GO!

DO NOT DISRESPECT MY WISHES.

LET'S MOVE.

ALL RIGHT, GUYS...

YES, SIR.

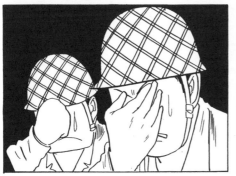

THAT NIGHT

MEANWHILE, THE SECOND PLATOON, HAVING PLUNGED ON IN THE DIRECTION INDICATED BY THE CAPTAIN...

PERHAPS THE ENEMY HAD BEEN LYING IN WAIT. THE MEN, BATHED IN THE ENEMY'S CONCENTRATED GUNFIRE, WERE UNABLE TO MOVE AT ALL...

HMM, GOOD IDEA.

SIR! MAYBE WE SHOULD PULL BACK TO CAMP AND ATTACK AGAIN AT A BETTER TIME.

LOOKS THAT WAY.

THE ENEMY MUST THINK WE'RE THE MAIN FORCE.

AAH

ENEMY TENTS RIGHT IN FRONT OF OUR CAMP...

WHAT ARE YOU SQUEALING LIKE THAT FOR?

THAT DOESN'T SURPRISE YOU?

AND IT'S ALMOST DAY AGAIN.

WHICH MEANS THAT WHILE WE WERE ATTACKING ONE ENEMY SECTION, ANOTHER WAS COMING UP FROM THE WATER.

RUMBLE RUMBLE RUMBLE

PSSSHH

THERE'S NO SENSE IN TRYING TO ATTACK DURING THE DAY.

I'M FEVERISH.

I'M FREEZING.

AAAAAH

PSSSSSSHH

PSSSSSSHH

...

HELL, I'M STARVING...

...HMM.

THEN WE CAN MAKE OUR FINAL ATTACK AFTER WE STUFF OURSELVES WITH FOOD.

SIR, WE'D LIKE TO GO DOWN TO CAPE ST. GEORGE TEMPORARILY.

EAT MY FILL BEFORE LEAVING THIS WORLD.

I WOULD ALSO LIKE TO...

THE SURVIVORS OF THE SECOND SECTION PROCEEDED DOWN TO CAPE ST. GEORGE, WHICH HELD ONLY TRAGEDY.

MOVE OUT FOR CAPE ST. GEORGE!

WE WILL TEMPORARILY RETREAT TO CAPE ST. GEORGE, AND THEN RELAUNCH OUR ATTACK.

TAT TAT TAT TAT
BAM BAM BAM BAM BAM

THE NIGHT OF THE SUICIDE CHARGE, THE DOCTOR WAS ALSO ATTACKED, BY A DIFFERENT ENEMY SECTION.

MM HMM.

BAM BAM BA... BA... BA...

DOCTOR, THE ENEMY'S ATTACKING!

THE DOCTOR DIDN'T KNOW HOW THEY ESCAPED.

EVENTUALLY, HE FOUND HIMSELF WALKING IN THE MOUNTAINS SOMEWHERE WITH THE WOUNDED MEN.

TAT TAT TAT TAT

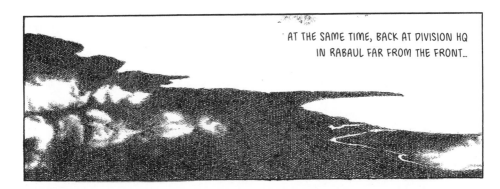

AT THE SAME TIME, BACK AT DIVISION HQ
IN RABAUL FAR FROM THE FRONT...

259

GENERAL!

WHAT DOES IT SAY?

HMM.

THERE'S A TELEGRAM FROM BAIEN.

"WE PRAY FOR THE GLORIOUS VICTORY OF RABAUL. MARCH 17TH, MAJOR TADOKORO."

"I WILL LEAD MY BATTALION INTO A SUICIDE CHARGE TONIGHT."

THAT GROUP SHOULD STILL BE ABLE TO FIGHT.

FROM THE INFORMATION WE'VE RECEIVED THUS FAR...

A SUICIDE CHARGE?

IT WOULD APPEAR SO, SIR.

TADOKORO'S YOUNG. LOOKS LIKE HE'S RUSHING TOWARDS DEATH.

SAY NOT TO RUSH INTO A SUICIDE CHARGE.

SEND A REPLY TO KEEP THAT CAMP ACTIVE AND FIGHT TO THE END...

KLAK KLAK

YES, SIR.

...

KLAK KLAK

WHAT?

SIR, BAIEN'S NOT RESPONDING.

DEAD?!

THEY'RE PROBABLY ALREADY DEAD.

THE FOLLOWING DAY, RABAUL

WHAT'S GOING ON?

MEN, STAND EASY.

ALL SOLDIERS, FALL IN!

AND NOW, THOSE MEN UNDER MAJOR TADOKORO HAVE MET THEIR DEATHS NOBLY.

THE MEN OF THE BAIEN BATTALION, WITH WHOM WE HAVE SHARED BOTH JOYS AND SORROWS, HAVE ADMIRABLY CARRIED OUT THEIR SWORN DUTY IN CONFRONTING THE SUPERIOR NUMBERS OF THE ENEMY.

HALF BOW TO THE LEFT! LEFT!

I'D LIKE TO HAVE A MOMENT OF SILENT PRAYER FOR THESE BRAVE MEN.

PRAY!!

HATS OFF!

FALL OUT!

HALF BOW TO THE RIGHT! RIGHT!

TADOKORO'S SUICIDE CHARGE HAS BEEN REPORTED AND THE GENERAL MADE THE ANNOUNCEMENT TO THE TROOPS HERE IN RABAUL.

GOOD TIMING, WHAT WITH DISCIPLINE FALLING OFF HERE.

THE NEWS OF THEIR DEATH HAS SADDENED EVERYONE.

WHAT HAPPENED NOW?

SIR, THE GENERAL WANTS TO SEE YOU.

SIR!

THE BAIEN MEN ARE NOT DEAD.

YOU WANTED TO SEE ME, SIR?

LOOK AT THIS. IT'S A TOP-SECRET TELEGRAM FROM THE POLICE IN CAPE ST. GEORGE.

WHAT?!

WHAT THE HELL IS THIS?

"THEY SHOW NO SIGN OF MOVING OUT SOON."

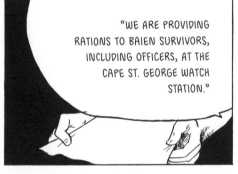

"WE ARE PROVIDING RATIONS TO BAIEN SURVIVORS, INCLUDING OFFICERS, AT THE CAPE ST. GEORGE WATCH STATION."

DESERTION IN THE FACE OF THE ENEMY!!

THEY'LL DISGRACE ALL OF US HERE IN RABAUL!

WE HAVE TO DEAL WITH THEM BEFORE THIS GETS OUT.

I'VE ALREADY REPORTED THEIR DEATHS TO HQ AND TO OUR TROOPS HERE. THIS IS SERIOUS.

LET ME HANDLE THIS, SIR.

SOMEONE IN A POSITION OF AUTHORITY MUST GO OUT AND TAKE CARE OF THIS.

YES, SIR.

I'M COUNTING ON YOU.

GOOD.

THEN MEET WITH THE LIEUTENANT-GENERAL TOMORROW.

THE LIEUTENANT-GENERAL IS THROUGH HERE, SIR.

RIGHT NOW, A GROUP OF SOLDIERS IS ATTEMPTING TO VIOLATE THE MILITARY CODE THAT IS MOST FUNDAMENTAL TO THE THOUSANDS OF TROOPS HERE.

THANK YOU FOR COMING.

REGARDLESS OF THE SACRIFICES.

ABOVE ALL ELSE, THE ORDER FOR A SUICIDE CHARGE MUST BE OBEYED...

THIS MISSION IS EXTREMELY IMPORTANT...

IF NOT, THE MENTAL FOUNDATION NEEDED FOR A DECISIVE VICTORY FOR RABAUL WILL CRUMBLE.

YES, SIR. WE ARE AWARE OF THE CONSEQUENCES.

AND ALSO VERY DIFFICULT.

YES, SIR.

ONCE THERE, YOU MAY USE WHATEVER MEANS NECESSARY TO ACHIEVE THIS OBJECTIVE.

270

CAPE ST. GEORGE

CHIRPING ABOVE
BIRDS IN THE SKY
TUMBLING FROM THE PEAK
THE ROAR OF THE WATERFALL

THE WAVES, LARGE AND SMAL[L]
MURMURING UNCEASINGL[Y]
THE SOUNDS OF THE OCEAN *

*SET TO A WALTZ TEMPO, "UTSUKUSHI TENNEN (BEAUTIFUL NATURE)" WAS WRITTEN FOR HIGH SCHOOL GIRLS TO H[...]

THOSE WHO MANAGE TO LIVE—AND WITH JOY AT THAT—DO SO AT THE PLEASURE OF THE GODS.

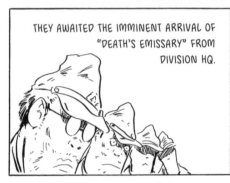

THEY AWAITED THE IMMINENT ARRIVAL OF "DEATH'S EMISSARY" FROM DIVISION HQ.

HOWEVER, THERE ARE MEN WHO SHOULD NOT BE ALIVE.

THE OFFICERS, WHO HAD THE GREATEST RESPONSIBILITY, STARED LISTLESSLY OUT AT THE OCEAN.

THE SOLDIERS RUBBED THEIR HANDS AND STOMPED ON THE EARTH AND PICKED THEIR NOSES, AS IF THEY FOUND IT STRANGE TO BE ALIVE.

THE COMMISSIONED OFFICERS WERE STILL STARING OUT AT THE SEA...

SUFFERING LIKE THIS, IT WOULD HAVE BEEN BETTER TO GO TOGETHER THAT NIGHT...

WHAT HAVE WE GAINED, BEING ALIVE STILL...

IT'S LIKE A LEAP, CROSSING FROM ONE PEAK TO ANOTHER.

BUT YOU KNOW, ISN'T THAT HOW LIFE IS?

IT'S THE WILL OF NATURE!

LIFE IS THE WILL OF THE GODS!

ANYTHING THAT GETS IN THE WAY OF THAT LEAP IS NO GOOD. WHETHER IT'S A SYSTEM OR WHAT HAVE YOU, IT'S EVIL.

NO! THE FACT IS, AS THE SENIOR OFFICER, I AM GOING TO GO TO THE GENERAL...

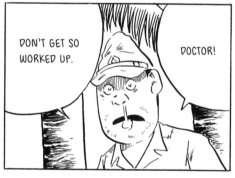

DON'T GET SO WORKED UP.

DOCTOR!

THEY THINK OF US AS WORMS AND NOTHING MORE.

DOCTOR, THAT'S OUTRAGEOUS...

AND PLEAD FOR THE LIVES OF THE EIGHTY-ONE SURVIVING MEN.

IT'S WRONG TO GET IN THE WAY OF THAT!

REGARDLESS, IT IS THE WILL OF THE UNIVERSE FOR ALL LIVING THINGS TO LIVE.

THIS 'ARMY' IS THE MOST DISEASED THING HUMANITY HAS EVER SEEN.

ARMY?

BUT THIS IS THE ARMY.

THIS IS NOT THE WAY HUMAN BEINGS SHOULD BE.

DOCTOR, DON'T GET SO WORKED UP.

WE KNOW NOTHING OF THE HEALTH OF THE CLEAR SKY, THE SINGING BIRDS, THE ISLAND NATIVES.

RATHER THAN SIT HERE AND WAIT FOR DEATH...

I AM NOT WORKED UP!

I'LL MAKE A LAST APPEAL FOR OUR LIVES.

DOCTOR, YOU CAN'T...

I'LL GET SOME SUPPLIES TOGETHER. GET ON A DAIHATSU* AND GO SEE THE GENERAL AT DIVISION HQ.

*A SHALLOW, BOXY BOAT USED BY THE JAPANESE IMPERIAL NAVY DURING WWII.

UNSWAYED BY THE PLEAS OF HIS COMPANIONS, THE DOCTOR BOARDED THE DAIHATSU.

281

THOSE FOOLS ARE PUSHING EVEN HARDER.

HMPH, AND ON THE DAY OF MY DEPARTURE...

YOU SEE THE DOCTOR FROM THE BAIEN GROUP?

VERY WELL.

SIR, I'M LEAVING FOR THE CAPE.

NO REAL PURPOSE IN IT, BUT HE CAME TO SAY SOME STUPID NONSENSE.

HAS HE COME HERE?

YES, SIR!

AND I'VE APPOINTED THE HEAD OF THE POLICE THERE THE LEGAL AFFAIRS LIEUTENANT.

TAKE HIM WITH YOU TO THE CAPE.

IN THE MEDIC'S UNDERGROUND SHELTER.

WHERE IS THIS DOCTOR NOW?

ARE YOU THE GENERAL, SIR?

WHY DID YOU COME HERE?

WHAT?

YOU'LL COME WITH ME TO CAPE ST. GEORGE TONIGHT.

YOU MAY SIT DOWN.

WHAT ABOUT YOUR WOUNDED?

THE DOCTOR FROM A SPECIAL ATTACK UNIT?

REPORT ON THE WAR?

I'M HERE TO REPORT ON THE PROGRESS OF THE WAR.

YOUR CASUALTY REPORT SHOULD BE CLEARER THAN THAT!

YOU'RE THE DOCTOR.

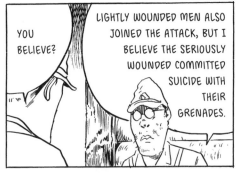

YOU BELIEVE?

LIGHTLY WOUNDED MEN ALSO JOINED THE ATTACK, BUT I BELIEVE THE SERIOUSLY WOUNDED COMMITTED SUICIDE WITH THEIR GRENADES.

YOU LEFT YOUR WOUNDED AND RAN AWAY, DIDN'T YOU?

AFTER THE BATTALION BEGAN THE CHARGE, THEY WERE ATTACKED BY ANOTHER ENEMY SECTION COMING UP FROM THE WATER.

SIR.

YOU IDIOT!

YOU CAME ALL THE WAY HERE TO REPORT THAT?

WE HAD NO IDEA WHO WAS DOING WHAT WHERE...BEFORE I KNEW IT, WE WERE WALKING TOWARDS CAPE ST. GEORGE.

FOOL!

I WAS NOT PERMITTED TO SEE HIM.

I CAME ALL THE WAY HERE BECAUSE I HAVE SOMETHING I WOULD LIKE TO SAY TO THE GENERAL.

WHAT IS THIS THING YOU HAD TO SAY?

IF YOU WERE IN FACT ABLE TO MEET WITH THE GENERAL, YOU WOULD ONLY FACE CHARGES AS A DESERTER.

I AM JUST A MAN WHO WILL JOIN YOU ON A DAIHATSU.

YOU'LL ONLY HIT ME IF I DO TELL YOU, SIR.

NO, I GIVE UP ON THAT.

COULD I ASK YOU FOR A CIGARETTE?

I AM REALLY SORRY FOR ASKING, BUT PERHAPS...

I WON'T HIT YOU, SO WHY DON'T YOU TRY ME?

I HAVEN'T HAD A SMOKE IN A MONTH NOW.

YOU DON'T EVEN HAVE ANY CIGARETTES?

TO BUY TIME.

AND ON TOP OF THAT, HAVE THAT BATTALION GO ON A SUICIDE MISSION?

SIR, WHY HAVE A SMALL BATTALION ATTACK A LARGER FORCE THEY CANNOT POSSIBLY WIN AGAINST?

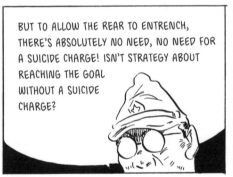

BUT TO ALLOW THE REAR TO ENTRENCH, THERE'S ABSOLUTELY NO NEED, NO NEED FOR A SUICIDE CHARGE! ISN'T STRATEGY ABOUT REACHING THE GOAL WITHOUT A SUICIDE CHARGE?

TO ALLOW THE REAR TO ENTRENCH AND MUSTER ITS FORCES PROPERLY.

BUT WHY, SIR? TIME FOR WHAT?

IMBECILE!

WHAT'S SO STRATEGIC ABOUT LOSING MEN WITH BRIGHT FUTURES IN A SUICIDE CHARGE?

288

YOU ARE A SOLDIER IN THIS ARMY! YOU WILL WATCH YOUR WORDS.

WHHAP

YOU ARMY MEN ONLY WANT TO BLINDLY KILL PEOPLE FOR NO REASON AT ALL.

I'M NO SOLDIER.

I'M A DOCTOR.

IS YOUR LITTLE WORM LIFE SO PRECIOUS?!

HOW DARE YOU!

STEP BACK AND TAKE A LOOK AT THE BIG PICTURE!

YOU'RE ALL MAD!

YOU DON'T VALUE LIFE AT ALL, DO YOU?

IN OTHER COUNTRIES, ARMIES ALLOW THEIR SOLDIERS TO FIGHT AND BE TAKEN PRISONER.

BUT, SIR...

WE CAN'T VERY WELL PLAN STRATEGIES BRIMMING WITH HUMAN EMOTION.

IT'S BECAUSE WE MUST CARRY OUT THESE SENSELESS SUICIDE CHARGES.

WHY IS THIS NOT PERMITTED IN OUR ARMY?

I ONLY RESPECT LIFE!

YOU SHAME YOUR COUNTRY!

WHAT THE HELL—

YOU THINK I'M NOT A MAN?

DO I SOUND LIKE A PANSY!

QUIT BEING SUCH A PANSY!

I'VE HAD MY FILL OF BEING HIT.

SIR, LET'S JUST STOP THIS.

IS THAT ANY WAY TO TALK TO A SUPERIOR OFFICER?

TAK

TAK

PFFT!

BANG

A MOMENT LATER, THE REPORT OF A SINGLE SHOT ECHOED THROUGH THE NIGHT.

?

KREE KREE

WE CANNOT BURY THE DOCTOR HERE.

YES, SIR.

DELAY MY DEPARTURE.

YES, SIR.

WE WILL CREMATE HIM AND TAKE HIS REMAINS TO BE BURIED IN CAPE ST. GEORGE, WHERE HIS SECTION IS.

KRACKLE
KRACKLE
KRACKLE
KRACKLE

EMISSARY OF DEATH

BEFORE LONG, AN UNINVITED GUEST ARRIVED IN CAPE ST. GEORGE.

HE'S GOT A WOOD BOX*.

IT'S THE CHIEF OF STAFF'S DAIHATSU!

*IN JAPANESE BUDDHIST TRADITION, THE DEAD ARE CREMATED AND PLACED IN A WHITE WOODEN BOX.

SIR, WHO
IS THAT?

THE DOCTOR!!

THE DOCTOR. I FELT HE SHOULD BE BURIED HERE WITH THE REST OF THE SOLDIERS.

HE COMMITTED SUICIDE.

WAS HE DISCIPLINED?

WELL THEN, I WILL SPEND THE NIGHT HERE.

THE PLACE WAS PUT TOGETHER RATHER QUICKLY, SO...

SIR, THE LIVING QUARTERS ARE THIS WAY.

THEY'RE LIVING IN THE HUT THEY BUILT IN THE JUNGLE.

NO, THIS PLACE IS QUITE GOOD. WHERE ARE THE BAIEN SOLDIERS?

YES, SIR!

GO AND TELL THE OFFICERS TO GATHER HERE.

YES, SIR!

DO NOT ALLOW THE ENLISTED MEN TO APPROACH.

YES, SIR.

NOW GET THE HELL OUT OF HERE!

THIS IS NO PLACE FOR AN ENLISTED MAN LIKE YOU.

WHAT THE HELL DO YOU WANT?!

AN IMPORTANT MEETING'S STARTING, ASSHOLE.

YES, UM, WELL—

DIDN'T I TELL YOU TO GET OUT OF HERE?

YOU'VE DONE WELL TO COME THIS FAR. GOOD WORK.

I'M LIEUTENANT-COLONEL KIDO.

YES, SIR. MY NAME IS YAMAGISHI. SECOND LIEUTENANT OF THE FIRST SECTION.

WHO IS THE SUPERIOR OFFICER HERE?

THE GENERAL HAS ORDERED ME TO COME AND TAKE CARE OF THINGS.

WE HAVE NONE, SIR.

WHAT ABOUT FOOD?

ENLISTED MEN IN TOTAL, SIR.

THERE ARE EIGHTY-ONE...

NONE, SIR.

SERIOUSLY WOUNDED?

THERE ARE TWENTY-SEVEN LIGHTLY WOUNDED, SIR.

LIGHTLY WOUNDED?

I WILL GIVE YOUR ORDERS AFTER THE INVESTIGATION IS COMPLETE.

AS TO WHAT COMES NEXT...

...

WHICH MEANS YOU ABANDONED THE SERIOUSLY WOUNDED, YES?

YES, SIR.

YOU WILL COME TO THE MAIN BUILDING ONE AT A TIME TOMORROW TO REPORT ON YOUR ACTIONS.

AND SO, THE FOLLOWING MORNING, LIEUTENANT-COLONEL KIDO BEGAN HIS INVESTIGATION.

IDIOT!

AND THE FACT THAT MAJOR TADOKORO DECIDED THE ENTIRE BATTALION WOULD ATTEMPT A SUICIDE CHARGE.

THE REASONS FOR THE BAIEN FAILURE WAS THE EARLY ABANDONMENT OF THE WARANGOE CAMP...

THE MEN BELOW ME WERE ALSO HUNGRY.

YES, SIR. I WAS VERY HUNGRY AND...

I'M ASKING YOU WHY YOU ENDED UP HERE.

I'M NOT ASKING YOU TO ANALYZE THE DAMNED WAR!

BUT WHEN WE ARRIVED IN CAPE ST. GEORGE, WE FOUND MANY OF OUR FELLOW SOLDIERS. WITH ALL THE OTHER MEN, I WAS UNABLE TO ORDER ONLY MY MEN TO RE-LAUNCH THE SUICIDE CHARGE.

YOU BEGGING BASTARD!

ANYWAY, I DECIDED THAT I WOULD ALLOW MY MEN TO EAT THEIR FILL, AND THEN WE WOULD RE-LAUNCH THE ATTACK.

YOU HAVE THE AUDACITY TO BE ALIVE, AND YOU STILL LOOKED FORWARD TO SEEING ME?

I HEARD YOU WERE COMING, SIR, AND I'VE BEEN WAITING FOR YOU.

YOUR SUPERIOR OFFICERS AND FELLOW SOLDIERS WENT INTO THAT ATTACK BELIEVING THAT YOU WOULD DIE ALONGSIDE THEM.

YES, SIR.

YOU REALLY HAVE SOME NERVE—ALIVE AFTER SUCH A BETRAYAL...

WHAT WILL YOU DO?

I'LL DO IT!

WHEN?

I WILL LEAD MY MEN ON ANOTHER SUICIDE CHARGE.

GOOD. YOU'VE MADE THE RIGHT CHOICE.

RIGHT AWAY, SIR!!

YES, SIR!

THAT'S THE RIGHT CHOICE, BUT I'LL GIVE YOU ORDERS ON THE TIMING LATER.

YES, SIR.

CALL IN SECOND LIEUTENANTS YAMAGISHI AND KITAZAKI.

WHAT I WOULD LIKE TO KNOW IS, ARE YOU PREPARED FOR WHAT HAPPENS NOW?

I FULLY UNDERSTAND THE REASONS FOR WHAT HAPPENED, BUT...

AND WHAT ARE YOU PREPARED FOR?

WE ARE PREPARED, SIR.

...

WELL, WE'LL TALK AGAIN TOMORROW.

...

NCOS, YOU'RE TO GO SEE THE LIEUTENANT-COLONEL IN ORDER OF SENIORITY.

QUIT YOUR JABBERING AND GET CRACKING ON THOSE PALM TREES!

DO YOU THINK HE'LL CALL THE ENLISTED GUYS?

NOW THE NCOS?

SHUT YOUR PIE HOLE! IT'S 'CAUSE OF THE MALARIA!

YOU LOOK PALE, SIR...

YES, SIR.

...

...I AM DEEPLY ASHAMED OF HAVING SAVED MY OWN LIFE. THE IMAGE OF MY FELLOW SOLDIERS IN THEIR LAST MOMENTS HAUNTS ME. I CAN'T SLEEP.

I AM DEEPLY SADDENED.

I CAN'T BEGIN TO EXPRESS MY REGRET OF HAVING SURVIVED.

ATTACK AGAIN BY MYSELF.

BUT I WAS UNABLE TO...

I WAS A COWARD.

I WISH I HAD DIED THEN.

THERE **IS** A WAY FOR YOU TO MAKE AMENDS FOR YOUR COWARDICE.

I WAS A FOOL!

I'LL DO IT!

YAAAH

I'LL DO IT!

STOP IT!

IT'S QUITE A DIFFICULT THING.

MAKING A MAN LAUNCH ANOTHER ATTACK AND DECIDE ON DEATH...

YES.

THIS IS REALLY A LOT OF WORK, SIR.

HMM.

HOW ABOUT SOME TEA, SIR?

HOW DID THEY SEEM AFTER THEY LEFT?

THE PROBLEM IS THOSE TWO OFFICERS.

SIR, SHALL I GIVE YOUR SHOULDERS A MASSAGE?

THEY ARE APPARENTLY MAKING PREPARATIONS, SIR. WRITING WILLS, THAT SORT OF THING.

ONE IS THE ONLY SON OF A RICH FAMILY, THE OTHER IS A TEACHER AT A GIRLS' SCHOOL.

WHAT DID THE TWO OF THEM DO BEFORE?

YOU'RE HARD AS A ROCK, SIR.

RUB RUB

I HAVE BEEN A LIEUTENANT FOR THE PAST FIVE YEARS.

SIR, I'D LIKE TO ASK YOU A RATHER STRANGE QUESTION.

HMM.

THAT IS A DIFFICULT ONE, ISN'T IT?

HMM.

I WONDER, SIR, IF THERE HASN'T BEEN SOME MISTAKE AT HUMAN RESOURCES.

OH! YOUR HEAD IS ALSO QUITE STIFF!

STIFF SHOULDERS MEAN A BLOCKED SPIRIT.

IN ORIENTAL MEDICINE, THEY SAY...

... ANYWAY, WHAT TO DO WITH THOSE TWO MEN...

OOPS!

HOMU, YOU'RE GOING TO TAKE MY EYES OUT!

OF COURSE, THEY ARE PATHETIC, BUT...

...

AS LONG AS THEY REFUSE TO ACCEPT DEATH AND JOIN THE ATTACK, I MUST DEAL WITH THEM ACCORDING TO MARTIAL LAW.

KREE
KREE

I AM NOT SO CERTAIN.

WHEN I THINK ABOUT THEIR FAMILIES...

THE FOLLOWING DAY...

MM HMM.

OH! HERE COME OUR TWO DILLY-DALLIERS NOW.

SIR, WE WILL COMMIT SUICIDE TO TAKE RESPONSIBILITY FOR OUR ACTIONS.

YOU MAY ENTER.

HOWEVER, YOU MUST CALL ME BEFORE YOU DO SO.

WELL DONE. YOU'VE MADE THE RIGHT CHOICE...

I'LL BE WAITING IN THIS HUT.

YES, SIR.

I HAVE SOMETHING I WOULD LIKE TO TELL YOU AS I WITNESS YOUR LAST MOMENTS.

IF THEY REALLY INTEND TO DIE, THEN I WILL HAVE THEM JOIN THE ATTACK.

SIR, WHAT ABOUT HAVING THEM ATTACK AGAIN WITH EVERYONE ELSE INSTEAD OF SUICIDE?

BUT IT'S ALREADY EVENING, SIR.

I AM WAITING HERE FOR THEIR DECISION.

I HEARD SECOND LIEUTENANT YAMAGISHI AND ANOTHER OFFICER ARE BEING FORCED INTO SUICIDE.

WHAT'S GONNA HAPPEN TO US?

SUICIDE? SUICIDE, DOESN'T SEEM REAL, HUH?

FORGET THAT. DID YOU BOIL THAT PAPAYA ROOT?

PROB'LY BAIEN.

WHERE?

RUMOUR HAS IT WE'RE ATTACKING AGAIN.

IT'S LIEUTENANTS YAMAGISHI AND KITAZAKI!

AND WE ENDED UP CAUSING YOU A PILE OF TROUBLE.

YOU GUYS HAVE BEEN A GOOD GROUP.

TO APOLOGIZE, WE HAVE DECIDED TO TAKE OUR LIVES.

YOU GUYS TAKE CARE, OKAY?

...

WE'LL TELL YOUR FAMILIES HOW COURAGEOUS YOU WERE.

PSSSSHH PSSS-SHH PSSSH

IT SEEMS THAT THE TWO LIEUTENANTS HAVE SAID THEIR GOOD-BYES TO THE ENLISTED MEN.

A BIT OF TROUBLE, SIR.

ARE YOU AWAKE, SIR?

THEY SHOULD'VE COME TO ME FIRST.

SO THE ENLISTED MEN KNOW THEN?

AND NOW THE SUN IS RISING...

PSSSSHH PSSSSHH

FROM MY MOM.

NO.

THOSE LETTERS FROM YOUR GIRL?

WHAT THE HELL WAS THAT SUICIDE CHARGE FOR...

PSSSSHH
PSSSSH

JUST SHUT UP, OKAY?

WHAT ARE WE KILLING OURSELVES FOR?

THIS IS OUR DESTINY, NO DOUBT ABOUT IT.

NO MATTER HOW MUCH WE KICK AND SCREAM, THERE'S NOTHING WE CAN DO ABOUT IT NOW.

PSSSH PSSSSHH PSSSSHH

THERE'S NO WAY AROUND IT, SIR. LET'S TAKE CARE OF THIS NOW.

THE DAY IS FULLY ON US, ISN'T IT?

PSSSSHH PSSSH

YES, SIR.

WE NEED TO FIND AN APPROPRIATE PLACE, SOMEWHERE DISCREET.

PSSSSHH PSSSSHH

...

NO ONE ELSE IS HERE. YOU MAY TALK FREELY.

IF WE KILL OURSELVES HERE...

WHAT IS IT?

SIR.

WHAT WILL OUR FAMILIES BE TOLD?

WILL THEY BE TOLD WE DIED IN COMBAT?

...

I FORMALLY APOLOGIZE.

WELL THEN...

I'LL MAKE SURE THEY ARE.

WE WOULD GREATLY APPRECIATE IT IF YOU WOULD BE SO KIND AS TO WITNESS OUR LAST MOMENTS AND TAKE CARE OF THINGS*.

*SEE NOTES PAGE 367.

I WILL TAKE MY LIFE IN ATONEMENT.

PSSSSHH

HOW ABOUT A LAST CIGARETTE?

FWOO

FWOO

EVERYTHING'S READY, SIR.

HAAH

FLICK

BANG
BANG

BURY THEM WITH THE DOCTOR HERE.

PSSSSHH PSSSHH

PSSSSHH PSSSSSHH

(RIGHT TO LEFT): SECOND LIEUTENANT YAMAGISHI; LIEUTENANT/DOCTOR; SECOND LIEUTENANT KITAZAKI.

CAPE MASSACRE

HEY! YOU CAN'T DRINK THAT WATER!

WHY?

WHAT AM I GONNA DO?

WHADDYA MEAN 'WHY'?! WHAT'RE YOU GONNA DO IF YOU GET AMOEBIC DYSENTERY!

WHAT'RE YOU TALKING ABOUT?

WHO CARES IF I GET AMOEBIC DYSENTERY?

OH YEAH.

WEREN'T WE JUST TOLD THIS MORNING THAT WE'RE DOING ANOTHER SUICIDE CHARGE?

THIS TIME'S FOR REAL.

FOR REAL?

WHENEVER THE CHIEF OF STAFF TELLS US TO GO.

WHEN'S IT GONNA BE?

YOU PLAN ON BEING THE ONLY ONE TO GET OUTTA HERE ALIVE?

OH HO!

I'VE GOT AKASAKI'S WILL AND STUFF FOR HIM...

WELL, I GUESS WE BETTER EAT UP THIS COPRA*.

*THE DRIED MEAT OF THE COCONUT.

ALL YOU NCOS DO IS GRUMBLE!

EATING SHIT LIKE THAT IS THE REASON YOUR WOUNDS DON'T HEAL.

LISTEN, THEY'RE BOMBING AGAIN.

WHAT?! I'M TRYING TO HELP YOU OUT HERE! I'M CONCERNED!

FIVE MEN?!

SIR, FIVE OF OUR SENTRIES DIED IN THE SURPRISE BOMBING.

WE HAVE TO MAKE THE ATTACK SOON.

I CAME HERE EXPRESSLY TO PREVENT THESE MEN FROM HAVING TO DIE LIKE DOGS, AND TO WHAT END?

THE GENERAL IS ALSO WAITING...

THREE DAYS LATER IN JUNE 1945, THE MAJORITY OF THE ENEMY'S FORCES BEGAN LANDING AT CAPE ST. GEORGE.

TAT TAT TAT TAT TAT

ASSEMBLE THE BAIEN SURVIVORS.

IT SEEMS THAT THE TIME FOR THE SUICIDE CHARGE HAS FINALLY COME.

YOU TAKE TEN MEN AND WAIT ALONG THE ROAD TO RABAUL. WATCH FOR ANY MEN TRYING TO ESCAPE LIKE THEY DID IN BAIEN.

YES, SIR.

I'LL TAKE THE COMMAND.

ON YOUR ORDERS.

IF YOU SEE ANY, SHOOT TO KILL.

ATTENTION!

SALUTE CHIEF OF STAFF KIDO! SALUTE TO THE FRONT, SALUTE!

ALL EIGHTY-ONE MEN ARE ASSEMBLED HERE, SIR.

AT EASE! SIR, WE HAVE EIGHTY-ONE MEN; FOUR ILL WITH MALARIA.

NCOS WILL LEAD SQUADS OF TEN MEN EACH.

WE WILL SURPRISE THE ENEMY WITH A REAR ATTACK AND FIGHT TO THE DEATH.

YES, SIR!

MIZUMOTO, WE WILL PROCEED TOGETHER.

BOW IN FAREWELL TOWARDS OUR BELOVED HOMELAND.

FIX BAYONETS!

SOLDIERS! BOW TO THE RIGHT! RIGHT!

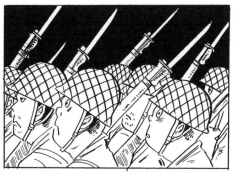

MOVE OUT!

GET
DOWN!

MEN, FIGHT THIS FINAL BATTLE WITH COURAGE!

ALL SECTIONS, ATTACK!

YA AAH

SIR?

MIZUMOTO,
I'M GIVING YOU
THE COMMAND.

IS YOUR SPIRIT FALTERING?

KEEP THE ENEMY AHEAD OF YOU.

TAKE COMMAND.

MY DUTY IS TO REPORT BACK TO THE GENERAL.

NO, SIR. AND YOU?

IT IS REGRETFUL, BUT I HAVE THE COLD DUTY TO SEE YOUR SUICIDE CHARGE OFF.

SO YOU WERE NOT PLANNING TO DIE WITH US, SIR?

BEFORE LONG, THE NIGHTMARISH
EVENING WAS OVER.

MARUYAMA REGAINED CONSCIOUS-
NESS WITH A START, AS THE EGGS
LAID BY FLIES IN THE BULLET HOLE
IN HIS CHEEK BEGAN TO HATCH.

WOBBLE
WOBBLE
WOBBLE

GUESS EVERYONE DIED FEELING LIKE THIS.

AAAH...

NO ONE TO TELL...JUST SLIPPING AWAY, FORGOTTEN...

WITH NO ONE WATCHING...

"WAS THE POSITION REALLY SO IMPORTANT THAT THEY HAD TO GO TO SUCH LENGTHS TO HOLD IT?"
—REGIMENTAL COMMANDER OF A NEIGHBOURING POSITION

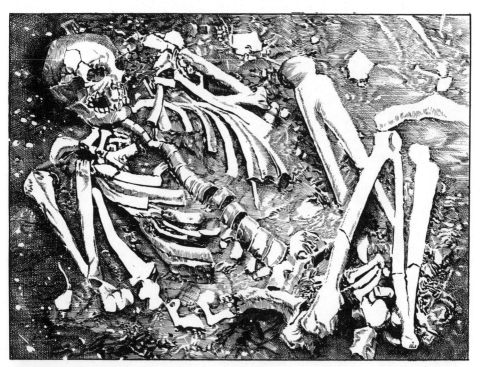

NOTES

29: Dai-Nanko was the name given to the 14th century samurai Masashige Kusunoki when he was taken up as a patriotic hero after the Meiji Restoration. He was used as an inspiration for suicide missions during World War II due to the fact that he sacrificed his life for the sake of Emperor Go-Daigo. The Battle of Minato River was a decisive battle which Kusunoki lost, leading him to commit suicide.

46: New Year's, or *Oshogatsu*, is possibly the most important holiday in Japan. It is a time to spend with family, much like Christmas in Western countries, with businesses and shops traditionally closed for the first three days of the year.

51: These cards, *hanafuda*, are a type of traditional Japanese playing cards. One set is made up of four cards featuring flowers for each of the twelve months of the year, for a total of forty-eight cards. Interestingly, the game company Nintendo originally formed to produce hanafuda cards.

59: Hokkaido is the Japanese island north of the main island of Honshu. The indigenous Ainu people there generally have more hair and lighter skin than other Japanese people, and have been discriminated against within Japan for centuries.

77: The Martin B-26 Marauder was an American World War II bomber manufactured by the Glenn L. Martin Company. The type's first combat mission was a raid on the Japanese base at Rabaul on April 5, 1942. Some of the Marauders operating in the South Pacific were fitted with an additional machine gun in the nose.

85: The military police, or *Kempeitai*, were the bane of many Japanese people's existence during World War II. Known as the Gestapo of Japan, the Kempeitai brutalized Allied prisoners and captured foreign women to serve as "comfort women" in Japanese brothels, but they also kept tight watch on the Japanese people themselves, harshly punishing even the slightest infractions.

108: This is a World War II army song. *Hanami* refers to flower-viewing parties, in particular to cherry blossom (sakura) viewing parties. Every spring, Japanese people go to parks to sit under the flowering trees and eat and drink and generally enjoy the delicate blossoms.

115: According to Japanese Buddhist tradition, the Sanzu River, similar to the River Styx in Greek mythology, separates the land of the living from the spirit world. The deceased must cross this river after death, but the manner of crossing varies with the life they led.

122: Burdock root (*gobou*), a popular winter vegetable in Japan, is tough and woody when raw, but soft and sweet when cooked. It is said that when prisoners of war in Japan were given burdock to eat, they thought the Japanese were feeding them wood.

125: Amitabha Buddha is the principal figure in the Jodo Buddhism sect popular in Japan. In Jodo Buddhism, a strong belief in the Amitabha Buddha is considered the key to salvation, and calling the Buddha's name over and over is believed to summon the Buddha to one's aid.

204: "Noble death" is the Japanese *gyokusai*, which is also the "Noble Deaths" of the title, *Soin gyokusai seyo! Gyokusai* is made up of the Japanese characters for "jewel" and "shattered," and became a euphemism for suicide attack during World War II. A more literal translation of *Soin gyokusai seyo!* would be "All hands, let's die honorably," with the idea that an honorable death was only found on the battlefield. Superior officers exhorted their soldiers with this phrase during the last phases of the war, when a Japanese defeat was becoming clear. Japanese soldiers were strictly instructed to die rather than be taken prisoner.

218: Harbin is a city in Northeastern China which was occupied by the Japanese during World War II. The city is in a province that borders Russia and, at the time, had a large Russian population.

221: *Kapporé* is a type of dance that originated near the end of the Edo Period. The final vowel here is changed from "ay" to "ee" to follow the rhyme scheme in the Japanese version.

223: This is a poem by Edo period writer Motoori Norinaga taken by Imperial Army soldiers as inspiration in World War II. "Yamato spirit" is the nationalistic ideal of the Japanese spirit and was often referred to during World War II.

245: The date of a person's death is very important in Japanese culture due to the various observances that must be carried out on specific dates after death. These observances depend on local customs, but are often held on the seventh day after death, then the forty-ninth, and then the hundredth day, followed by annual services or services in set years.

326: In this kind of ritual suicide, the person committing suicide is generally expected to cut his abdomen while a second, or *kaishakunin*, stands behind him to finish the job so that the person committing suicide does not suffer unduly. Traditionally, this second cuts off the head of the suicide victim in a ritualized manner, but in modern times, the second usually shoots the suicide victim in the head.

AFTERWORD

Shigeru Mizuki

Such lengths to hold that place...

Onward Towards Our Noble Deaths is 90 percent fact. The narrative has the chief of staff hit by a stray bullet and dying, and that is not true—he escaped quite handily at just the right moment. And in the story, everyone dies, but in reality, about eighty men survived.

You can't say to some members of a detachment, "We're all going to die later, so you guys go ahead and die now." No one would willingly accept that. I suppose all *gyokusai*, or suicide charges, are like this; there are always survivors. But the thing is, on Peleliu*, almost no one survived, so that became the standard. Those of us in Rabaul were often told to model ourselves after Peleliu. And if we had been on an island like Peleliu where everyone could die all at once, our suicide charge would have succeeded. But in the case of Rabaul, with a hundred thousand soldiers living quite comfortably at the rear, you can tell five hundred soldiers (maybe three or four hundred in reality) on the front to die, but you definitely won't get those five hundred men to consent to that.

In our military, soldiers and socks were consumables; a soldier ranked no higher than a cat. But when it came to death, it turns out we were human beings after all. "Even a worm will turn," as the old saying goes, and I believe that a suicide charge simply can't succeed without the tacit agreement of every soldier in the group.

Our newly assigned 27-year-old battalion commander may have been a wonderful guy when you got to know him, but he was much too young to command nearly five hundred men, each with his own individual will. The "chief of staff" was the one who gave the commander this order, rather than leaving him to come up with a suicide charge on his own, likely because the division commander above him was planning to tell the hundred thousand Rabaul soldiers, "Die here," and he intended to turn us into an example.

NEW RECRUITS ARE LIKE TATAMI MATS: THE MORE YOU BEAT THEM, THE BETTER THEY ARE.

YOU GET THE MES-SAGE?

Officers, NCOs, horses, soldiers: in the military hierarchy, soldiers were not even thought of as human beings. We were instead creatures lower than a horse. I wonder if surviving the suicide charge wasn't, rather than an act of cowardice, one final act of resistance as a human being.

In this story, everyone dies in the end, but I originally wanted one soldier to escape and report to the commander of the regiment holding the neighboring position. But it would have gotten too long, so I had everyone die in the suicide charge. The general in charge of the third mixed regiment actually said this about our suicide charge: "Why did they have to go to such lengths to hold that place?" All I could do when I heard this was heave an empty sigh.

Such lengths to hold that place... What vain words these are, the dead have no mouths to tell.

Whenever I write a story about the war, I can't help the blind rage that surges up in me. My guess is, this anger is inspired by the ghosts of all those fallen soldiers.

Shigeru Mizuki
August 1991

*Translator's note: Peleliu is the island in the South Pacific where one of the bitterest campaigns of World War II was fought. A campaign that was expected to last four days dragged on for over two months, and resulted in some of the U.S.'s worst casualty rates. Most of the Japanese on the island were killed. An estimated ten thousand nine hundred Japanese soldiers were killed and 302 people taken prisoner, but of the prisoners, only seven were soldiers and twelve sailors. The rest were non-Japanese labourers.

Q & A with SHIGERU MIZUKI

This written interview was conducted in February 2011, a month before Shigeru Mizuki's 89th birthday, with the invaluable assistance of Maki Hakui, Christopher Butcher, and Jocelyne Allen.

Drawn & Quarterly: You've used your cartooning and status to address the war, starting with themes in *Akuma-kun*, and moving to aggressively criticizing Japan's role in World War II, and war in general. What prompted you to begin directly addressing Japan's role in the war with your manga?

Shigeru Mizuki: I've drawn a variety of war manga, but with *Onward Towards Our Noble Deaths*, what prompted me was the feeling that I wanted to leave a record of this significant event. My thoughts about war have not changed.

D&Q: Was there anything, beyond your personal experiences, that inspired you to create a graphic novel on the war? One of the extraordinary aspects of this book is that, when it was first published in 1973, there were virtually no other graphic novels, in any country, taking on such a serious subject with this level of ambition and scope. Were you aware at the time that this was such a groundbreaking work, not just in Japan, but in the world as well?

SM: I wasn't aware that it was a pioneering work. I was just single-minded in my desire to write it.

D&Q: In your afterword for this book, you note that the events recounted here are "90 percent fact." Was there anything from your experiences in the war that you felt that you could not include in this book, either because it was too sensitive politically or because it compromised the privacy of any of the other survivors from your group?

SM: There was nothing in particular that I hesitated to write about.

D&Q: You note that, unlike the ending portrayed in this book, about eighty men had, in fact, survived the battle. Have you maintained a friendship with any of your fellow survivors?

SM: I haven't had much contact with my war buddies since I came back to Japan. The ones that I was really close with all died in the war.

D&Q: The landscapes and overall scenery portrayed here are masterfully drawn and characterized by an intense realism. What sort of visual references did you use? Was this primarily drawn from memory (or reference photographs) or at any point did you travel back to the island of New Britain?

SM: I ran into my former commanding officer from the front at work, which led me to visit Rabaul after twenty-six years. That ended up being what made my desire to leave a record with *Onward Towards Our Noble Deaths* so strong. The details in the book are mostly from memory, but I also used some photographs and things from when I visited.

D&Q: What sort of critical reception did *Onward Towards Our Noble Deaths* receive in Japan when it was first published?

SM: It didn't really get that much attention, actually.

D&Q: You were one of the first artists to attempt to do serious, non-fiction manga with your biography of Adolf Hitler in 1971. Was doing this biography a step towards doing your own autobiographical works, which are still somewhat rare in Japan?

SM: I was intrigued by Hitler. There's no relationship between my writing about Hitler and my autobiographical works.

D&Q: What has formed the basis of your cultural influences? What other manga, films, books, etc., have inspired you?

SM: My influences cover a wide range of things, and I can't specifically point to one. It's probably better to answer that I don't have any.

D&Q: Your body of work appears to stand out beyond much of the manga that has come out of Japan over the last thirty years or so. In particular, books such as *Onward Towards Our Noble Deaths* and *NonNonBâ* are distinguished by an intense personal vision that seems uncharacteristic of much of contemporary commercial manga. Do you feel that your work shares a greater affinity with other *manga-ka* [Japanese cartoonists] of an earlier era? Do you read any current or recent manga works?

SM: I don't feel there is any affinity with any particular manga-ka. I don't read recent manga.

D&Q: How long did it take you to write and draw this book? Was it serialized in any form (magazines, newspapers) or was it published upon completion as one entity?

SM: It took almost no time to plan it. I finished writing it in a short period. My strong feeling of wanting to write it, of needing to write it, forced me to do so.

D&Q: In your career as a manga-ka, you have tackled a wide range of subject matter, from the events in this book that relate to your own experiences in the war, to the supernatural elements in *Akuma-kun* and *NonNonBâ*, to the biography of Hitler. Do you have a work that you are most proud of? For English-speaking readers encountering your work for the first time, what other books after *Onward Towards Our Noble Deaths* would you recommend?

SM: I would have to say *GeGeGe no Kitarô*.

D&Q: It would be something of an understatement to say that your work is long overdue for publication in English. Given the scope of your influence and accomplishments in Japan, it's very surprising that this is the first time that your work is being translated into English. How do you feel about *Onward Towards Our Noble Deaths* being published in North America for the first time?

SM: I'm extremely happy about it. I hope readers will come to understand the feelings of the Japanese soldiers fighting on the foremost lines of the battlefield.

This book is presented in the traditional Japanese manner and is meant to be read from right to left.

To begin reading, please flip the book over and start at the other end. Read the panels (and the word balloons) from right to left—starting from the top right corner.